The Earth's Surface

Physical Geography in Colour

D. C. Money, M.A., F.R.G.S.
Head of Geography Department, Bedford School

Evans Evans Brothers Limited London

Published by Evans Brothers Limited
Montague House, Russell Square, London, W.C.1.

First Published 1970.
Reprinted 1970, 1972.

By the same author:
Patterns of Settlement: Human geography in colour.

Printed in Great Britain by Thomas Nelson (Printers) Ltd.,
London and Edinburgh

237 28648 3   2770

Contents

Introduction

Most people have an interest in the natural scenery which is part of their everyday life and travels. Wherever we journey, as layman, budding geographer, or more advanced student with an eye for familiar landforms, the raw material is all about us—shapes and surfaces which have evolved over long periods of time and which are still continuously changing. A study of the evolution of the landscape features can be most rewarding; although the origins of many landforms are still not certain, and informed conjectures and fresh theories are frequently being put forward. This is part of the fascination of examining the earth's surface: it is always possible to ponder how this or that combination of features has come about; and, as we observe and measure the processes by which landforms evolve, the more interesting it is to speculate, with some confidence, on their origins.

There are, of course, many parts of the earth—tropical, polar, desert, mountainous—which we may have little opportunity of inspecting at first hand. Visual aids now play an important part in teaching; but most of these are transitory displays, removed after a short period. This book provides more permanent visual aids, especially through the use of numerous colour photographs, with their accompanying annotated sketches—the kind of simple outline sketch one might make to record significant features in the field—and, alternating with these, the pages of text and diagrams which help to explain the physical processes themselves.

The abundance of illustrations allows the book to serve students of a wide range of age and ability. With this in mind, the text is simply written; and although terms with which a student of Advanced Level geography should be familiar are used, they are explained both in the text and captions, so that less advanced students may understand them.

The concept of 'age', as in Davis' 'cycle of erosion', is explained, but qualified by reminders of those processes which cause infinite variety in actual landforms, such as the creation and removal of rock-waste, and base-level and climatic changes. Simple quantitative field-work will soon convince students that the 'cycle' concept has many limitations.

Most of the photographs have appeared in series prepared by the author for 'Pictorial Education' and have been specially taken to illustrate particular landforms; gaps in my own coverage have been filled from the collections of colleagues to whom I express my gratitude—particularly to Miss J. A. Somerville, Mr. P. Conway, Mr. I. D. Taylor, and Mr. K. G. Fish, for their help and advice in assembling the illustrations.

Acknowledgment is due also for the cover photograph and the photographs forming Figs. 51, 118, 125, 126, 164, 177, 195, 196, 200, 232, 245, 246, by Eric Kay; Figs. 128, 129 from Paul Popper Ltd; and Figs. 49, 95, 96, 190 by courtesy of the High Commissioner for New Zealand.

D.C.M.

Part I Formation and Destruction

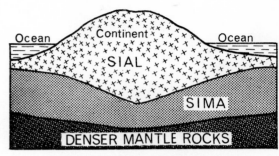

Fig. 1. The visible continental mass and its 'roots'.

The Earth's Structure

It is about 4,000 miles from the outer crust of the earth to its centre. This solid outer crust extends down for some 3 to 20 miles, being thickest beneath the continents.

Fig. 1 shows that an outer layer of lighter granitic rock, with a sedimentary covering in places, (p. 4), appears to rest on a denser mass, much of which is similar to basalt (see below). The outer rocks have a high proportion of *si*lica and *al*umina (*sial*); those beneath contain much *si*lica combined with *magnesia* (*sima*).

Beneath these, extending far down to the heavy core of the earth, are the still denser rocks of the *mantle*; in the upper parts, at high temperatures, and under great pressure, these have acquired 'plastic' qualities which enable them to flow very slowly.

This book deals with the surface rocks and surface structures, and it is sufficient simply to point out that as the continental land surfaces are worn down, movements can occur, far beneath the surface, which may cause the 'deep-rooted' continental mass to rise in adjustment—in the way that a wooden block floating in water would rise if a weight were removed from its top. This is but one of the many causes of movements which take place in the earth's crust.

The Earth's Crust

As the earth cooled, the surface was initially composed of *igneous* (fire-formed) glassy or crystalline rocks. The drastic actions of expansion and contraction, and the effects of storms and, later, of running water caused the surface rocks to break up into particles of various sizes; these were then blown or washed into hollows or carried into the first seas. These ever-continuing processes of disintegration and transportation of the broken material, through weathering and erosion, are described below (pp. 12-15).

In the four to five thousand million years which have followed, as these processes have continued, innumerable surface features have been worn down and new ones created; and earth movements have raised both the old worn surfaces and the rocks newly formed by one or other of the processes considered in the following sections.

Igneous Rocks

These have cooled from the molten state, and contain minerals in a form which depends on their origin and rate of cooling (see Fig. 2).

When molten *magma* is forced to the surface and extruded, rapid cooling produces either rocks with tiny crystals, as in the dark brown or black basalt (B), or else glassy rock, like obsidian (O).

In general, rocks cooling slowly beneath the surface have larger crystals; rocks such as granite (G), formed in huge masses at depth, tend to be coarse-grained, with crystals of visibly different size and colour.

1

Igneous and Metamorphic Rocks

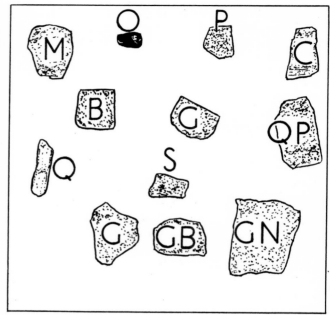

Fig. 3.

Fig. 2. Crystalline rocks, mostly formed by igneous action. The rock textures are affected by pressures and temperatures at which they form; crystal size is generally small if the cooling is rapid. The mica and the pure, clear quartz (Q) are mineral constituents of granite. (C—the 'odd man out' has crystalline bands slowly formed from solutions.)

M —Muscovite Mica; splits into thin, pearly crystal 'plates'

O —Obsidian; quickly cooled 'volcanic glass'

P —Pumice; light with cellular structure; gas-filled lava which cooled rapidly

B —Basalt; heavy, basic, brown-black, once quick-flowing, lava with small crystals

G —Granite; slowly cooled at depth, with visible quartz and coloured crystals

GB—Gabbro; coarse-grained, basic; no quartz

S —Syenite; coarse-grained, deep-formed, with no quartz

QP—Quartz-porphyry; large quartz crystals in a mass of fine-grained igneous rock.

GN—Gneiss, crystals banded by heat and pressure.

The Texture of Rocks

The physical and chemical make-up of a rock affects its behaviour when exposed to the changing weather conditions. Some igneous rocks, like the granites opposite, have many large crystals of various colours, with different heat-absorbing properties and different coefficients of expansion. Changing temperatures may thus set up stresses and strains which help to make them disintegrate. Their crystals may also have different solubilities or water-retaining properties, which may also weaken the rocks, and perhaps cause them to break-up.

The nature of coarse-grained rocks, such as that in Fig. 4, makes them vulnerable to these processes; and when exposed as an isolated relic mass in a tropical wet/dry seasonal climate, such as that of the savannah lands, allows exfoliation (described in more detail on p. 12). The peeling off of outer 'shells' of rock leads to the consequent rounding of the projecting feature, as seen in Fig. 4.

There are many other examples in the pages which follow of the effects of atmospheric heat and moisture on various types of rock. It is obvious, therefore, that the composition of the rock has much to do with the characteristics of landforms and of scenery as a whole.

Fig. 4. Relics of hill-masses of close-textured, coarse grained rocks stand out on the plateaux of Tanzania; sometimes, as this, isolated and rounded by weathering (p. 12), sometimes of the castle-like 'kopje' type (Fig. 122).

3

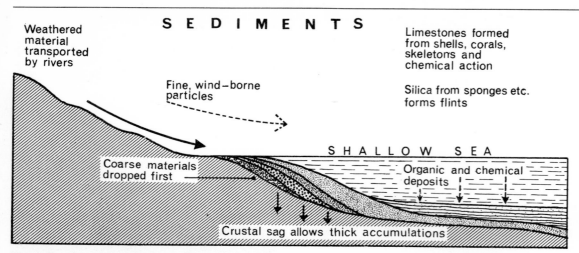

SEDIMENTS

Weathered material transported by rivers

Fine, wind-borne particles

Limestones formed from shells, corals, skeletons and chemical action

Silica from sponges etc. forms flints

Coarse materials dropped first

SHALLOW SEA

Organic and chemical deposits

Crustal sag allows thick accumulations

Fig. 5. Conglomerates, sandstones, and limestones in the making.

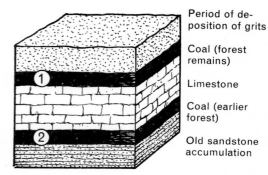

COAL SEAMS

Period of deposition of grits

Coal (forest remains)

Limestone

Coal (earlier forest)

Old sandstone accumulation

Fig. 6. At the base of the coal seam (1) may be thin sandstones of the swampy basin.

Sedimentary Rocks

Sedimentary rocks are formed from materials which have accumulated as the result of various processes: by the build-up of particles derived from other rocks, or from the remains of organically formed matter (from living or once-living things), or from deposits created by chemical action.

'Mechanically Formed' (Clastic) Rocks

When rocks break up, the particles may be transported, the finer ones by wind, others by water in the form of boulders, gravel, coarse or fine sands, or of much finer silt or clay, to a place where they may collect and build up great thicknesses of material.

Rivers carry mineral particles into shallow seas. The coarse material is shed first, the finer carried further out. Under great pressure of the accumulations above them, the layers compact in time to form *sandstone* rock. Those of angular grains are generally called *grits*, and may have been wind-borne rather than transported by water. Layers of coarse pebbles are sometimes cemented together by limy matter to form *conglomerates*. The finer material forms sandstones which vary greatly in composition and hardness, and some may also be cemented by chemicals into hard rocks.

Organically Formed Rocks

Some of these are formed in seas from the shell or skeleton remains of sea-creatures. They may be shell collections cemented together, or accumulations of millions of tiny skeletons, with some larger ones, or a mixture of these with calcium carbonate formed chemically in the water. Rocks resulting from these processes are called *limestones*; chalk is a soft limestone. Some organisms, however, have a silica skeleton, which, after change, provides the material for *flint*, so often found embedded in carbonate masses like chalk, (p. 7).

Slowly decomposing plants produce much carbon. Over the years they may build up layers of dark, soft fibrous material called *peat*, or a more compressed form known as *lignite* (brown coal). Severely compressed remains of ancient swamp forests remain as layers, or seams, of *black coal*, bedded in other rocks (Fig. 6).

Chemically Formed Rocks

Calcium carbonate may be precipitated chemically from lime-rich waters. The small grains may eventually build up rocks like *travertine*; and probably the great thicknesses of *oolite* limestone (with its small, rounded egg-like particles) were built up from such accumulations.

Other salts may accumulate by evaporation from salt lakes or shallow seas; like the sodium nitrate in Chile's inland basins, they may be commercially valuable.

Subsequent Changes in the Rocks

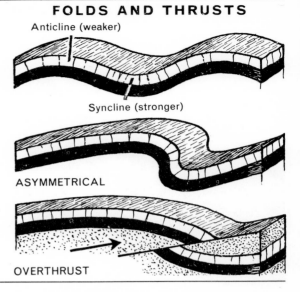

FOLDS AND THRUSTS

Anticline (weaker)

Syncline (stronger)

ASYMMETRICAL

OVERTHRUST

Fig. 7. Some common contortions.

Metamorphic Rocks (A Change in Form)

In time, rocks may become subjected to high temperatures and pressures, and their composition altered chemically or physically. The intrusion of very hot igneous matter is a common cause of such *metamorphic* change in the adjacent rocks.

Sandstones may be turned to *quartzites*, clays and shales to harder, brittle rocks with visibly different recrystallised minerals. The minerals of granite occur in irregular bands in hard, metamorphic *gneiss*. Pressure may cause fine clay particles to become layered, and under intense pressure to form *slate*, with the minerals lying in parallel 'cleavage' planes, at right angles to the direction of compression; heat and pressure together may convert a limestone into *marble*. There are numerous types of metamorphic rock in which heat, pressure and chemical activity have combined to create changes.

The Age of Rocks

In sedimentary rocks, built up in sequence, layer upon layer, the dominant life-forms of each period of geological time may be revealed by their fossil forms—of mammals, reptiles, amphibia, fishes, invertebrates, and plants.

A time-scale may be worked out comparatively for the rocks in which they occur, with the help of various modern techniques. For instance, rocks may now be dated by the relative proportions of radioactive materials, and of the products of their decomposition, which are found to be present—the rate of radioactive decay being known.

Some igneous rocks may be so dated; and their age may also be estimated by their presence and position among other rocks of a known period.

Fig. 119 shows a sequence of sedimentary rocks in an area in which the age of primitive man and his artifacts, locally discovered, could be related to that of the rock strata in which they were found.

Crustal Movements

We have only to look at the folding of rocks—relatively gently displaced like those in Fig. 16, or severely distorted as in Figs. 232 and 233—to realise that crustal movements can exert great forces of compression and tension.

Folding may be severe or otherwise, and can result in contortions which are symmetrical or asymmetrical (Fig. 7). The downfolds, *synclines*, tend to be structurally strong and compressed, and upfolds, *anticlines*, under stress and weaker.

Severe pressures or tensions may result in cracks or *faults* (p. 8). Fig. 7 shows how a *thrust* may so displace folded rocks that one limb of the fold overrides another. This may give rise to abrupt changes in the surface scenery as rocks of different ages are brought into contact.

Crustal movements are not always dramatic or rapid. Many surface features are due to periods of slow uplift or depression (p. 60).

5

Sedimentary Rocks: Sandstones

Sandstones are formed from the accumulation of fine or coarse materials, and may have been laid down by one or more processes. The materials from which many sandstones are formed have been carried by rivers and deposited in shallow seas. There they have grown in thickness as layer upon layer of the compressed sediment accumulated.

River-borne pebbles are generally rounded. In Fig. 8 you can see the smooth pebbles embedded among the thick material of varying size which was transported and then deposited by a river. After great thicknesses had accumulated, the river and its tributaries cut deeper into the landscape, leaving the pebbly alluvium as terraces far above (p. 40). 'Alluvium' is the name given to accumulated water-borne material.

The materials in Fig. 8 are loosely bedded; but many sandstones, under the pressure of rock above, or by chemical processes which cement their grains, have become very hard indeed.

The wind may transport small particles, which usually become angular in the process; so that sedimentary rocks which have been formed from these accumulations, when perhaps desert conditions prevailed, can be identified as such by the nature of the particles.

Fig. 8. River terrace gravel overlying a bed of much finer alluvium exposed on the banks of a tributary of the River Loire in central France.

Sedimentary Rocks: Limestones

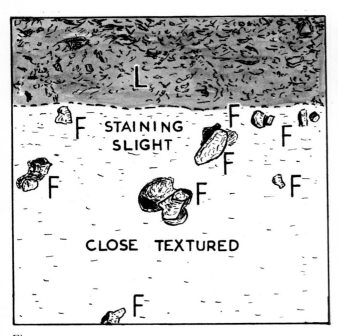

Fig. 9.

Chalk is a soft limestone, which in temperate, moist climates gives rise to a gentle topography, whose characteristic features are described more fully on p. 25. Notice, in Fig. 10, the close texture of this porous rock.

Amid the thicknesses of calcium carbonate building up on the sea beds tens of millions of years ago were the remains of sea organisms, like sponges, composed partly of silica. With time, the silica—once in a mobile 'colloidal' form—became re-deposited in cavities (sometimes slowly replacing once-living matter), in the form of flint nodules, or, in the latter case, as moulds of the original substances, or fossils.

Fig. 10. Chalk with flints (F) in a cutting in the Chiltern Hills. In the upper layers (L) it is stained by solutions from the soil; it also shows the reddish tinge imparted by iron compounds, concentrated in soils derived from such chemically basic rocks.

7

Rock Distortions

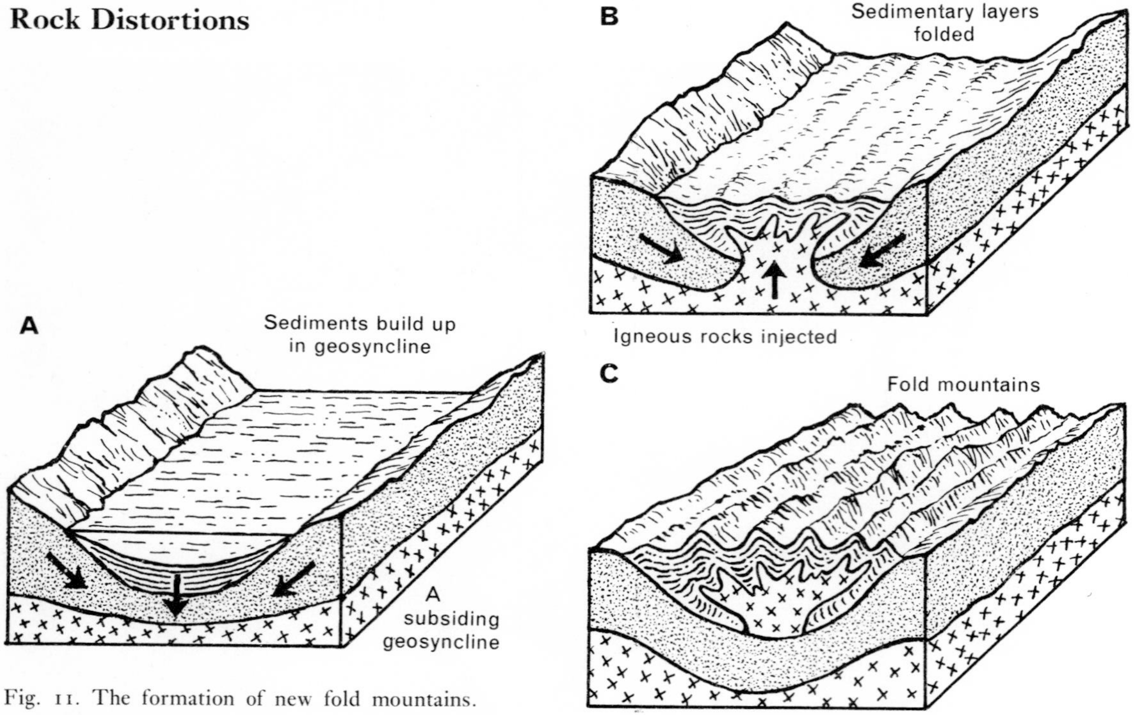

Fig. 11. The formation of new fold mountains.

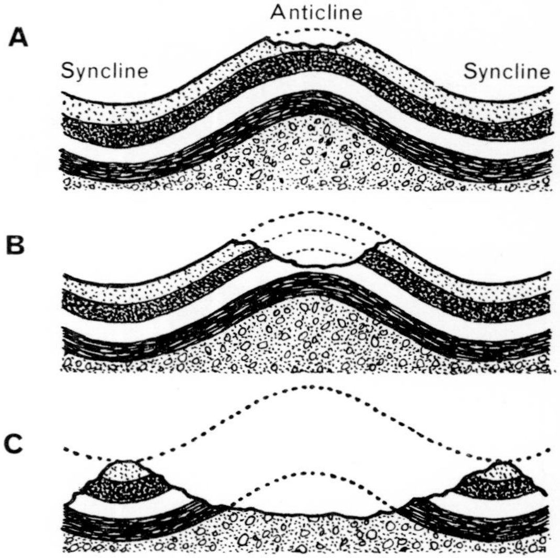

SYNCLINAL MOUNTAINS

Fig. 12. The progression from upfolded heights to mountains with the rocks downfolded.

Fold Mountains

Deep-seated movements cause some parts of the earth's crust to warp downwards into large basins (geosynclines). In these, sediments may accumulate, and by their own weight tend to cause further subsidence. Fig. 11A shows that the whole downward movement may cause the land-masses bounding the geosyncline to move inward, and molten material from the depths may intrude into the sedimentary rocks, as in B.

The ultimate result is that the contorted sediments are thrust up in the form of *fold mountains*. Beneath them lie the intrusive granitic rocks in great masses, known as *batholiths*, as in C.

The forms of the mountains themselves are very complex, with over-thrust ranges along the edges of the adjoining land areas. Also, of course, they in turn, from the moment of formation, are acted on by the agents of weathering and erosion (pp. 12-15).

In some cases rocks contorted into synclines may eventually come to form mountains. The adjoining weaker upfolds (p. 5) are exposed to erosion, so that their rocks are easily worn away. As the crests are removed, valleys are created between inward facing scarps (Fig. 12A). These high valleys may then acquire active river systems, which in turn widen and deepen them, as in B.

C shows that, finally, the landscape may include *synclinal mountains*.

Faulting

When forces are tending to move the crust, either vertically or horizontally, the compressions and tensions may cause cracks and fractures, against which the rocks are displaced; these are known as *faults*.

Fig. 13 shows normal faults, vertically and inclined, and how forces of compression also cause dislocation along a thrust (or reversed) fault. Fig. 13 also shows a tear fault, in which horizontal displacement has occurred.

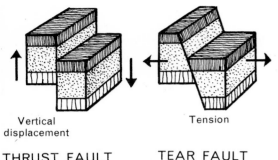

Vertical
displacement

Tension

THRUST FAULT **TEAR FAULT**

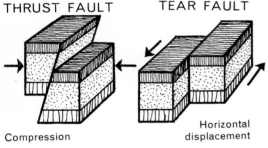

Compression

Horizontal
displacement

Fig. 13. Movements along fault faces.

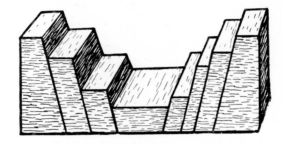

Fig. 14. Diagrammatic view of a step-faulted rift valley.

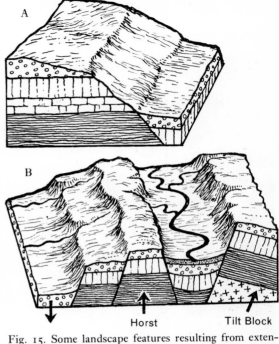

Horst

Tilt Block

Fig. 15. Some landscape features resulting from extensive faulting.

Rift Valleys

These long depressions, lying between parallel faults, may extend for hundreds of miles. The great rift system running from the Middle East to the Zambesi is over 4,000 miles long, and includes the deep troughs of the Dead Sea, the Red Sea, and many of the East African lakes.

The sides of these valleys are frequently step-faulted, as shown diagrammatically in Fig. 14. In nature, of course, weathering and erosion greatly modify the boundary faults—see Figs 15 and 42; but even so the walls and trough can be remarkably impressive, as in the case of the eastern rift near Nairobi (Fig. 19).

Volcanic outpourings (p. 108) are often associated with extensive faulting and with rift valleys. Earthquakes are also apt to occur in regions of fault development.

Faulting and the Landscape

The effects of weathering and erosion are discussed later in the chapter. Their combined actions continually modify the landscape, so that what may appear to be simple features when shown diagrammatically, as in the fault diagrams, are not always easy to recognise in the field.

However, faulting does produce outstanding features of the landscape, which we should be

prepared to recognise as such. Even so, to recognise a simple fault scarp, as shown in Fig. 15A, may call for careful investigation in the field; for there are many causes which may have produced an abrupt scarp-face of this kind.

In B, the landscape is more dramatic. Upthrusts have produced flat-topped block mountains, or *horsts*, and also an outstanding tilted block. There has also been down-slipping along fault faces. But, again, in time, even this landscape may be so modified that its origins are not obvious.

9

The Bedding and Folding of Sedimentary Rocks

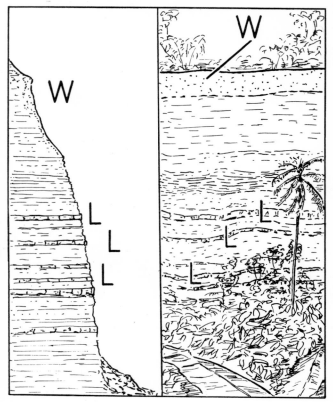

Fig. 17

Massive slips from steep tropical hillsides, undercut by a river, expose gently folded sediments (their bedding seen in profile in Fig. 17). Soil and weathered material (W) readily falls, leaving scars. The whole region is prone to earth movements and faulting.

Other pictures showing how the folding and tilting of sedimentary rocks affect the contours of the landforms and coastal features are: Figs. 24, 42, 138, 226, 229, 232, 233, 245.

Fig. 16. Sedimentary strata exposed in Buff Bay River valley, northern Jamaica. The horizontally bedded rocks have been folded into gentle waves, shown up by the thicker limestone bands (L).

Faulting and Rift Valleys

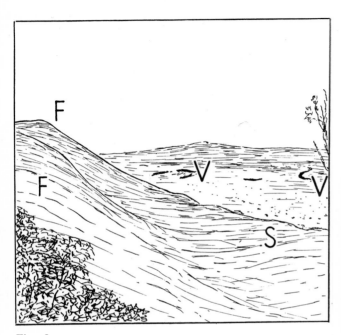

Fig. 18.

Fig. 19. The Eastern Rift Valley in the Highlands of southern Kenya—one of the branches of the immense rift valley system which runs south from Syria for many thousands of miles, and includes the Red Sea and many of the East African lakes.

Here the faulted edges (F) of the highland stand above the wide, level surface of the rift valley, more than a thousand feet below. With time, the rock falls and screes (p. 12) have come to mask the lower angles of slope (S) of the valley sides, formed as the edges themselves are worn back. Here, as is so often the case, the lower slopes of mixed minerals and newly formed soils are well wooded, in contrast to the open savannahs beyond.

The rift valley contains the remains of many extinct volcanoes, and on the nearer side of the valley signs of past igneous activity are seen in the low residual rock formations like those at V.

EXFOLIATION

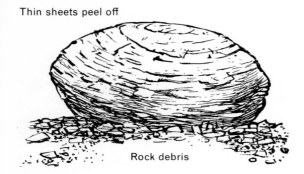

Thin sheets peel off

Rock debris

Fig. 20. The combined effects of strong heating and chemical action.

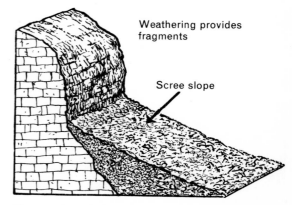

Weathering provides fragments

Scree slope

Fig. 21. Combined action of weathering and gravity.

Weathering

Every day physical and chemical processes act on the existing landforms exposed to the atmosphere, breaking them down into 'weathered' material, which may be removed by wind or water and perhaps redeposited elsewhere.

The effectiveness of each type of weathering depends on the rock structure, climate, vegetation cover and other factors.

Among the processes which break up the rocks is the alternating *expansion and contraction* caused by high surface heating by day and rapid cooling at night. In fact, *chemical action* often speeds up this process; even in deserts water in the form of dew may allow chemical action, or else produce stresses by hydrating and so enlarging crystals. In deserts and dry tropical grasslands, where the surfaces become very hot when exposed to the sun, a combination of these processes causes thin, irregular layers to peel off—a type of weathering called *exfoliation*.

Frost action may also cause rapid break up; for when water in a crack freezes and expands, it exerts great pressure within the rock. Joints are opened, and fragments may be detached from steep faces of well-jointed rocks. *Gravity* is a constant force which aids weathering, as fragments fall to collect at the base of cliffs, exposing new faces to the atmosphere, but also protecting the base.

The debris which collects at the foot of such slopes is called *scree*. The angle of the scree slope depends on the rate of accumulation and removal of material, and on the shape and size of the fragments.

Plant roots and *animals* burrowing into the rock face also help disintegration; although the spreading roots of vegetation may act as a binder of otherwise loose material, and so prevent soil erosion.

Chemical Weathering

Apart from the effects of hydration and the changes in crystal size, water, if slightly acid, as is rain water, dissolves and carries away in solution many minerals, including calcium carbonate, of which the bulk of limestones is composed, (p. 21). Plant acids may also cause the 'rotting' of rocks. The oxygen of the atmosphere oxidizes some minerals and, by changing their composition, may weaken the whole rock structure.

Transport of Materials

Among the agents which move weathered material away from the bed-rock, and so prevent a 'waste mantle' from protecting the rock, are gravity, wind, and moving water. The latter may be in the form of rills, streams, rivers, sheets of water, ice, and, along the land margins, the sea.

These various forms of transport, and the features resulting from the subsequent deposition are described in later chapters. The balance between the accumulation and removal of waste tends to vary, of course, from season to season.

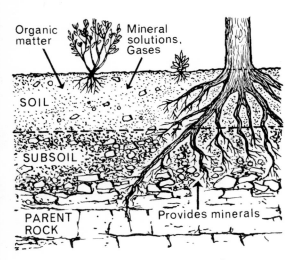

Fig. 22. Soil; subsoil; and the parent rock.

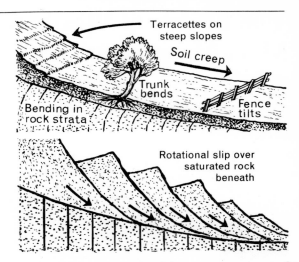

Fig. 23. Two processes involving mass movements of surface materials.

Soil Formation

The continual breakdown of particles derived from the bed-rock produces the solid mineral contents of that most important material—soil. By itself, this mineral matter is *not* soil; for other processes and constituents are involved in the formation of the soil itself. It is, however, the parent material. Air and moisture are contained between the mineral particles, and also a vegetable and animal population, which includes minute organisms, such as bacteria, and the products of decomposition of the organic, once-living, contents.

The composition of the soil varies as the elements of climate act upon it over a period of time, during which it gains or loses various constituents.

Soil, therefore, does not depend on the nature of the bed-rock alone; and indeed soils of very different characteristics may develop upon the same type of rock in different parts of the world. However, the bed-rock and the local topography do have powerful influences upon the nature of the soil and its depth. Fig. 22 shows the relationships between the bed-rock, the sub-soil, which contains much coarse material weathered from the rock, and the true soil above.

Erosion

In a sense, *erosion* is the wearing away of the land; but it is generally distinguished from weathering as being the process of land destruction by those agents which remove the debris at the same time— as do moving ice, running water, or wind armed with sharp sand particles; many examples are to be found in the pages which follow.

Mass Wasting

Soil and sub-soil may move bodily down slopes by means of a slow creep under gravity; or by the flow of water-logged material; or by sliding or slumping, which may leave great scars on a hillside. The more insidious effects of creep are often seen in the bending of trees and fences, or even the upper parts of rock strata.

Natural occurrences may aid the movements of stones and small soil particles down-slope. Rain may wash fine material away from stones, which are then free to roll. The soil itself may expand as its water content freezes, so that stones are heaved up to the surface. Animals burrowing, or even moving along a slope, may cause soil and sub-soil movements; and man's actions may bring about relatively rapid displacements, as when ploughing turns the soil always in one direction relative to the slope.

The sudden movements are apt to take place in particular localities, as where a layer of clay lies beneath a loose sandstone, which may become waterlogged with prolonged rain. The slips shown in Fig. 23 should not be confused with faulting. The latter involves movement along a fault face which extends deep into the rocks beneath.

The Effects of Weathering, Gravity, and Mass Movements

Fig. 24. The exposed grits of Mam Tor in the southern Pennines of western Derbyshire, with evidence of the actions of weathering and gravity, and of mass slips from the rock face.

Fig. 25

The grits of the southern Pennines lie above clays or shales, and the springs at the base of the grits are among the causes of the many slips which occur along the joint planes: some of them leave great scars on the hillsides.

In Fig. 24 the mounds at L are part of former landslips, now grassed over. Above, the high scree slopes (S) are built from materials which have been loosened by weathering from the steep exposed face of the dark sandstones.

Displaced rocks may often be heard rattling down the face, and Mam Tor has been nicknamed the 'Shivering Mountain'.

Surface Erosion

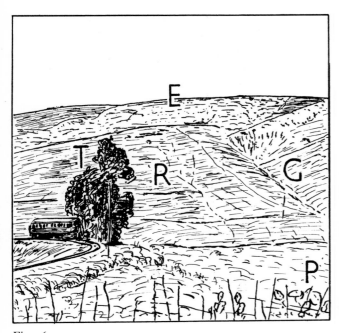

Fig. 26

Fig. 27. Young wheat grows on a badly eroded hillside (E) in southern Sicily. During the summer the soils dry out, which makes them the more vulnerable when winter storms cause run-off. The aridity is emphasised by the presence of prickly pear (P).

Here run-off has caused, and is still causing, severe erosion on loose sandstones. Notice the deep gulley (G) and the scars at its head, where soft rock slips away from the steeper slopes. Even beneath the young wheat, the rills at R have begun to join to form a new gulley system, just visible through the crop.

The trees (T) are Australian eucalypts, well able to withstand long dry periods; they are often used as wind-breaks in Mediterranean lands.

Alternating wet and dry seasons, especially where there are steep slopes and poorly consolidated rocks, lead to soil erosion in many other parts of the world, such as the drier parts of the Monsoon Lands.

Part II Ground Water and River Systems

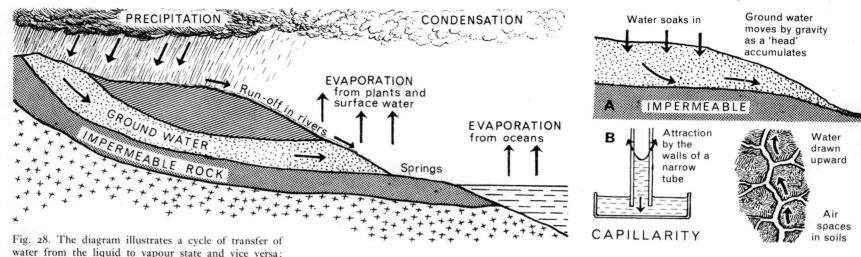

PRECIPITATION CONDENSATION

Water soaks in | Ground water moves by gravity as a 'head' accumulates

EVAPORATION from plants and surface water

Run-off in rivers

GROUND WATER

IMPERMEABLE ROCK

EVAPORATION from oceans

Springs

A IMPERMEABLE

B Attraction by the walls of a narrow tube

Water drawn upward

CAPILLARITY

Air spaces in soils

Fig. 28. The diagram illustrates a cycle of transfer of water from the liquid to vapour state and vice versa; but water may be held for short periods in vegetation and for much longer periods in ice and snow, or as ground water in the rocks themselves.

Fig. 29. In A the water soaks in. B shows that the molecular attraction of the containing solids may elevate water in soils as in a tube.

The Water Cycle

Water mainly enters the atmosphere by evaporation from moist surfaces, from oceans, rivers, moist ground, snow caps, and vegetation. After condensation, it may be returned to the earth, mostly in the form of rain, snow, hail, or dew—collectively known as 'precipitation'.

Rain falling onto a surface either runs off, evaporates directly, or soaks into the soil or surface rocks. Some is held for a time in the soil or vegetation; some moves underground through rock pores and cracks.

Effects of Rock Structure

Rocks with small spaces between grains or nodules are said to be *porous*, and capable of soaking up water like a sponge; many, but not all, sandstones are porous. Jointed rocks, or those with many cracks like hard limestones and granites, may not be porous, yet allow water through these openings, and are said to be *pervious*.

Any rock which allows water to pass through it is *permeable*. Conversely, those, like clay, whose fine grains are so packed that water cannot permeate them, are said to be *impermeable*.

As we have seen already, some, like the hard limestones, may be non-porous but allow water through joints and are thus pervious: in addition they may also be soluble in acid rain water, and hence very vulnerable at the joints, which tend to be enlarged (p. 21).

This has a great effect on the nature of local landforms. Water will run over the surface of impermeable rocks and almost certainly follow channels, which become ever deeper, so that, in time, a network of valleys may break up the surface of the landscape (p. 32). Porous rocks, on the other hand, may absorb water, so that there is much less running over the surface, which remains relatively unbroken by valley systems (p. 30). The extent to which the processes takes place must depend on the nature of the climate.

Ground Water

Water which soaks into rocks moves downwards under the force of gravity. However, it may also be caused to move up any fine 'tube' (as formed, in a sense, by the interlinking passages between soil particles), by capillary attraction (Fig. 29). In this way water may be drawn up and evaporated from the surface.

16

The Water Table

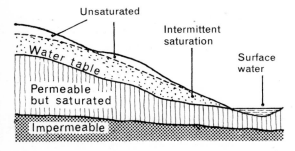

Fig. 30. Zones in the permeable rock depend on the balance between rainfall, evaporation, and water issuing from within the rock.

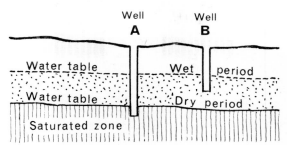

Fig. 31. The different seasonal heights of the water-table.

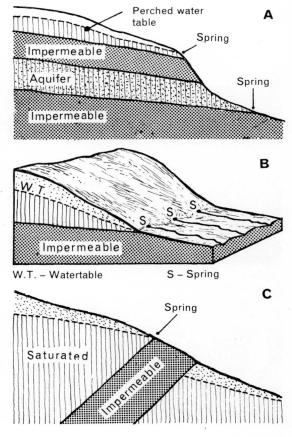

W.T. – Watertable   S – Spring

Fig. 32. A, B, and C show three ways in which water held above impermeable rock may emerge as springs.

Saturation

Fig. 30 shows that water may soak in and move downward through pores and joints until it meets impermeable rock. It then fills the spaces in the lower parts of the permeable rock, gradually causing the whole mass to become saturated with water up to a level known as the *water-table*.

Above the water-table there is an intermittent zone which may or may not become saturated, depending on the quantity of water soaking in and retained. High parts may never become saturated.

The downward movement under gravity means that the water-table tends to be far below the surface near the hill-top, but near the surface at the foot; while in the valley ground water may seep out (as in Fig. 32) and so stand at, or run off, the surface. A 'head of water', of course, exerts a pressure which increases with its height, and this pressure acts in all directions, so forcing the water below through permeable rocks.

Wells

If a hole is dug deep enough to extend below the water-table, ground water seeps from the rocks into the well. Wells tend to retain water according to the depth of the water-table and the 'head of water'. If the level of the water-table drops sufficiently, either seasonally or permanently, a well may dry up.

Fig. 31 shows that, whereas well A has water even in the dry season, well B will hold water only when the level rises during a wetter period.

Springs

Ground water moving through a permeable rock under the force of gravity and the head of water at the higher parts of the water-table, may issue from hillsides as *springs*. (A water-bearing rock is termed an *aquifer*).

The Nature of Jointed Limestones

This organically formed well-jointed rock shows *stratification*—that is to say it reveals divisions between the layers (or strata). The plane of these divisions is known as the *bedding-plane*, and here it is almost horizontal. Fig. 35 also shows the plane surface revealed by erosion.

Compare the texture of this form of limestone with that of the soft, porous limestone, chalk—seen in Fig. 10.

Small particles of clay or sandy material may form impurities which, cemented into the calcium carbonate, help to make it non-porous and increase its resistance. Many of the English Midland limestones contain iron salts, which give them a characteristic red-brown appearance.

The faces of these massive blocks of limestone show the close texture of the hard non-porous rock. The water is unable to soak through the mass of the rock, as it does into soft chalk; but the many cracks and joints enable surface water to find its way far below the ground, passing vertically and horizontally through the rock. At the same time, as the water seeps slowly through, it dissolves part of the calcium carbonate, and so widens the openings.

Fig. 33. A quarry in the mountain limestone near Wirksworth in the Derbyshire Pennines where the rock is almost horizontally bedded. It also shows clearly the many joints which are typical of this form of limestone, and which play a large part in forming characteristic features of limestone scenery.

Swallow Holes in Carboniferous Limestone

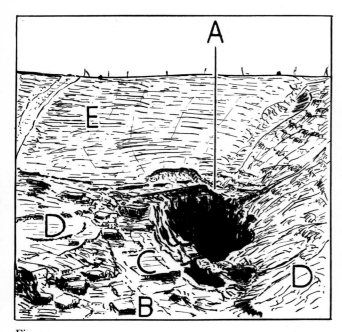

Fig. 34

The surface once concentrated the rainfall run-off so that it collected in a wide hollow, where the effects of solution became pronounced. In time solution-widened joints, and chasms formed below, allowed blocks of rocks to fall in, and so leave a hole at the surface. The water which sinks in now moves through underground passages and emerges as a beck from Ingleborough Cave.

Notice the shaft entrance (A); the loosened, jointed blocks (B); the bedding-plane revealed at C; the prominence of the edges of the bedded blocks affecting the profile of the slopes (D); and the *terracettes* (E) formed on the steep grassy slopes opposite by the slow, downward slipping of the soil material.

Fig. 35. Gaping Ghyll, a huge swallow-hole at Ingleborough in the Pennines in north-west Yorkshire. The opening leads downwards for 365 feet, and into a cavern over a hundred yards long and more than a hundred feet high. Notice the scale, given by the protective fencing.

Springs

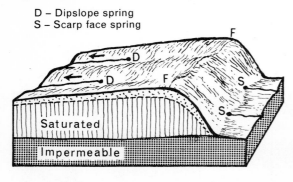

D – Dipslope spring
S – Scarp face spring

Saturated

Impermeable

- - - - - - - - Water table

Fig. 36. The water-table is low beneath the higher parts of the escarpment, but valleys may be sufficiently deep to tap the water-table some way down the dip slope.

ARTESIAN WATER

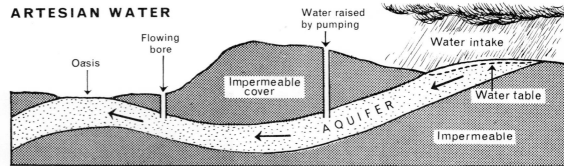

Oasis

Flowing bore

Impermeable cover

Water raised by pumping

Water intake

AQUIFER

Water table

Impermeable

Fig. 37. The aquifer shown may lie far beneath the surface. Water from artesian sources, coming from considerable depth, is often hot and, dissolving minerals from the rocks, may have become saline, though not necessarily.

Impermeable rocks which impede the movement of ground water may cause a rise in the water level, so that springs issue from a 'perched water-table' on its up-slope side (Fig. 32A).

Water may also seep out along a line at the cliff face in the circumstances shown in Fig. 32B. But usually the irregularities at the junction of the permeable and impermeable rocks cause the water to issue as springs at specific points.

The photographs and diagrams, Figs. 59–62 on pp. 34, 35, show how a spring may develop on the sloping face of a rock mass (here a pebble ridge) when water moves through the permeable body of the 'hill' feature. In this case this is the rather unusual circumstance of water moving through a barrier beach (p. 140) from an unusually high pond held back by the ridge under flood conditions.

Fig. 36 shows the development of springs on the dip-slope of an escarpment. These emerge at points DD, where the water-table rises above the floor of the old valleys. The valleys themselves

may have been cut during a wetter period, or else developed when the retreating scarp FF was much in advance of, and higher than, its present position. At the foot of the escarpment a 'spring-line' exists, with streams flowing forward from springs SS. The water emerging may create valleys in the scarp face by a sapping process, followed by a collapse of rock above the point of emergence.

This is again illustrated by the unusual case of the massive pebble ridge in Fig. 62, where the whole sapping process proceeds very rapidly.

Water may emerge in other circumstances: in the case of the artesian water (Fig. 37) and, at intervals, in the form of hot geysers (p. 28). When the water circulates to great depths it may become heated and so emerge as hot springs. Springs frequently deposit dissolved minerals about their place of issue, building up mounds or terraces of salts. Limestone, in the form of travertine, is commonly built up in this way.

Artesian Water

In some cases a permeable aquifer is sandwiched between impermeable rocks in such a way that rainwater may sink into the permeable rock where it forms part of the surface. It may then percolate downward through the aquifer, to form a reservoir of what is known as *artesian water*.

An artesian well may be drilled, into which water flows under pressure of the head of water below the highest part of the water-table (Fig. 37). Under these conditions, water may gush forth from the artesian bore—or emerge at an 'oasis' where the rock of the aquifer is again exposed.

Where sufficient pressure is not created, pumping may be necessary to raise water to the surface, as in Fig. 37. Here it can be seen that the well-head on the high ground is above the level of the water-table in the aquifer; so that natural pressure cannot force water to the surface.

Limestone Scenery

Fig. 38. Solution hollows lie along the now dry stream bed. Dark lines indicate likely paths taken by water beneath the surface.

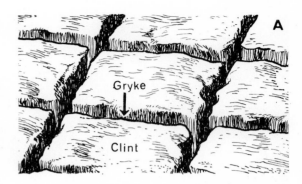

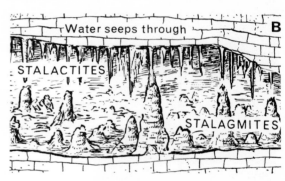

Fig. 39. Solution is responsible for the 'pavement' formation of clints and grykes (A); redeposition in caverns beneath may take the forms shown in B.

Rain-water is a dilute solution of carbonic acid, formed from atmospheric moisture and carbon dioxide. Soil water may also gain acid characteristics from decaying plant matter. So that, initially, the water which soaks into the rocks is often acidic.

Limestone rocks are mainly composed of calcium carbonate, sometimes with much magnesium carbonate. They cover a large part of the earth's surface, and are particularly vulnerable to corrosion by acid. Dilute carbonic acid converts their insoluble carbonate into soluble bicarbonate, which may be carried away in solution.

Hard limestones are not porous but pervious, and water passing frequently through the many joints enlarges them by solution. Beneath the surface, the water continuing to pass down and along cracks and joints may in time create underground caverns, familiar in Britain to pot-holers in the Carboniferous Limestones of the Pennines and Mendips.

Along the courses of surface drainage channels, the water may disappear through cracks which eventually become larger and deeper and develop into *sink holes* (Fig. 38). Collapse may leave gaping holes, partly filled with debris (p. 24).

Beneath the surface the caverns are often vast, with clayey floors, from impurities in the limestone, and contain icicle-like *stalactites* hanging from the roof, or thicker *stalagmites* rising from the floor. These result from the redeposition of insoluble carbonate, formed as water slowly seeps through the roof and evaporates, or drips and scatters on the floor beneath, building the pendants and columns by slow encrustation.

Trickles of water down the cavern sides produce fluted forms. Sometimes complete pillars are formed as stalactites and stalagmites are united.

At the surface, the enlarged joints may become deep grooves, or *grykes*, separated by furrowed blocks with ridges, or *clints*.

Ground Water Emerges

In the course of downward movements through the joints in the limestone, the water may in time form caves and underground channels within the limestone mass, perhaps as far down as an impervious rock beneath. At certain places the water may emerge as springs (p. 20), or, as here, in the form of an underground stream, the headwaters of a system of surface drainage.

Here a waterfall has developed as the stream flows across the bedding planes and tumbles over the jointed rock faces. The latter are cut and worn back by the action of the fall itself (p. 65).

This stream emerges from amidst the limestones which make up the Jura Mountain system of the French-Swiss borderlands. (The name 'Jurassic'—describing the geological period of time—derives from these mountains).

Fig. 40. Headwaters of the River Loue flowing from an underground cavern in the Jurassic limestones of eastern France.

Abandoned Surface Channels and Underground Flow

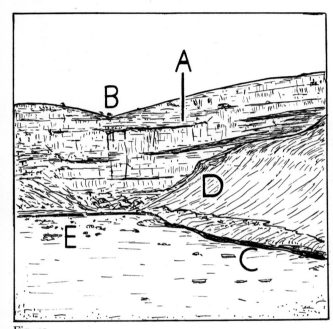

Fig. 41

Here again are features due mainly to the marked jointing (A) and the solubility of the Carboniferous Limestone.

Faulting has produced a series of scarps, and the weathering of the limestone has produced sheer faces of the kind seen in this picture.

As there has been much removal of exposed rock since first the faulting occurred, with a retreat of the rock face, such a feature is known as a *fault-line scarp* (rather than a *fault scarp*).

The spring at the foot of the cove which gives rise to the stream (C) is not that which disappears further up the valley, seen as a high surface feature at B, but is fed by water sinking elsewhere in the limestone. Notice the slope of debris at D and the limestone blocks at E.

Fig. 42. Malham Cove in the Yorkshire Pennines—a cliff nearly 300 feet high. A spring of water gushes from the foot and runs through the green hollow beneath; but, once, a high-level stream followed a valley across the surface and plunged over the face as a waterfall at B.

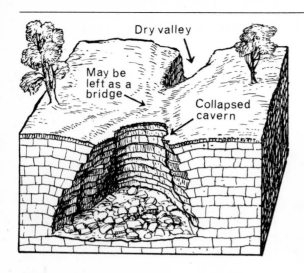

Fig. 43. Multiple collapse—a typical 'Karst' feature.

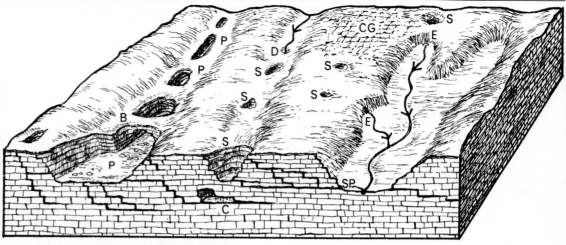

S – Sink hole   SP – Spring
B – Natural bridge   E – Stream emerges
D – Disappearing stream   CG – Clint gryke surface
P – Flat-floored valley (Polje)   C – Cavern

Fig. 44. Some of the many features to be seen in a landscape evolved upon hard, jointed, but soluble limestones.

Cavern Collapse

A series of cavern collapses may lead to the formation of long narrow valleys, floored with the broken limestone blocks, and sometimes may result in the creation of a natural bridge—the last vestige of a former surface or cavern roof.

Karst Topography

The Karst region of the limestone plateaux of Jugoslavia, to the north-east of the Adriatic Sea, exhibits so many examples of sink-holes, valleys formed by collapse, dry surface valleys, and dramatic piles of limestone blocks or broken limestone pavements, that it has given its name to topography of this kind.

In the basins formed by collapse or by solution, there is often a soil, particularly valuable for agriculture in such desolate country, which is made up of the accumulation of impurities left as the limestones dissolved. When occurring on Mediterranean limestones, under the prevailing climatic conditions, this clayey soil is often bright red and known as *terra rossa*.

Many of these features are shown diagrammatically in Fig. 44. In such countryside, surface streams may disappear and, after passage underground, reappear at the surface lower down—though not necessarily along the line of the former surface drainage, indicated by the dry valleys on the present surface (see Figs. 42 and 46).

Eventually, having created the disjointed, broken ridge and basin countryside seen in Fig. 44, these processes may act to remove the entire limestone cover and, in fact, leave a region of low relief.

Thus there is created a kind of 'cycle of erosion' typical of Karst country. In this there is downward movement, through solution holes, of water from the streams, while other streams continue to flow in normal valleys; then a period when some streams are still at the surface, some seasonal, depending on the height of the water-table, and some have disappeared, leaving dry valleys. At this time, certain rivers may cut down rapidly and take water from valleys higher up—though others, as in Fig. 44 may flow at the surface, perhaps in clayey basins, and receive water from springs at the valley sides. Finally, however, underground streams may reach underlying impermeable rocks; so that, when the Karst surface of collapsed cavern roofs and remnant blocks is removed, there is once more surface drainage.

Chalk Topography

Chalk is a limestone, but a soft one, and, unlike the harder varieties, is porous. Water can thus soak

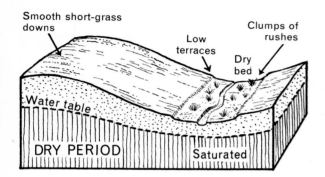

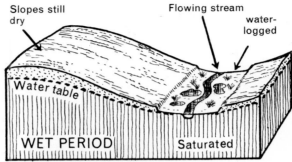

Fig. 45. Many chalk streams appear only when the water-table rises after a wet period.

into the mass of the rock, so that surface run-off is usually slight. For this reason, the rills and stream valleys (p. 32), which are characteristically developed by running water on the surface of the non-porous rocks are few.

Because of the scarcity of small drainage valleys in most chalk country, the outline of chalk hills tends to be smooth and regular (Fig. 52). Where, for one reason or another, valleys have developed, their profile is usually gentle, compared with the steep-sided valleys developed in the harder, more jointed limestones (Fig. 46).

In fact, the various types of chalk rocks vary in their hardness and contents: impurities left in the form of tiny insoluble particles, as the carbonate is removed, accumulate to form a clay. Also, as seen in Fig. 10, silica deposits, formed together with the carbonate, may have been converted into flint, and flint nodules often form marked bands

within the chalk. Solution of the chalk often leaves a residual soil of clay-with-flints, capable of supporting very different forms of vegetation (and crops) than the chalk itself. Sometimes bedding planes are clearly visible in chalk, and the presence of joint planes are often responsible for the almost vertical nature of many chalk cliffs. On the other hand, the uniformity of the thick chalk rocks also tends to bring about a regularity of cliff retreat under erosion, (Fig. 216), and is largely responsible for the regular gentleness of the hill features already referred to.

The chalk mass as a whole is affected by chemical weathering, and solution hollows also develop in chalk where water is concentrated for some reason and moves regularly through the rock. Slips and slumps, with their resulting scars, are also to be seen on chalk, especially on steep slopes close above an impervious rock.

Valleys and Bournes

The deep, broad, gentle valleys in chalk downland may have been created at a time when the rainfall was greater than at present, or when the subsoil in front of the Ice Sheets (pp. 100-104) would have been permanently frozen, so that water flowed strongly over the surface.

Seasonal streams, or *bournes*, responding to changes in the level of the water-table, are features of many chalk valleys. Fig. 45 shows how a long period with little rain may so lower the water-table that the river bed dries up in its small flood plain (p. 40), on which only the presence of rushes or coarse grasses indicate that the soil is usually very wet. After a wetter spell, the water-table rises, so that the bourne carries water and ponds may lie on the now marshy valley floor.

Fig. 55 shows many water-cut features on a now dry chalk upland.

25

The Dry Surface of a Jointed Limestone

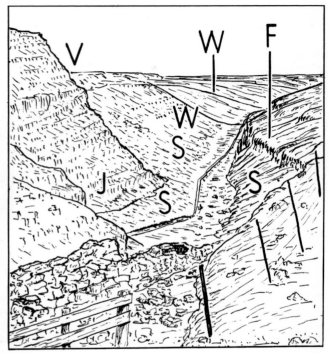

Fig. 47.

At times there have been much moister surface conditions. The water-table must, for instance, have remained high for a long period as Britain's ice cover (p. 100) slowly vanished. Surface water flowed in deep valleys in many parts of the Pennines which now bear little surface drainage.

Notice the walls (W) emphasising the line of the valley and the slopes; the steepness of the valley sides (V), typical of valleys in hard Carboniferous Limestone, and the 'free faces' (F) where blocks have fallen from the jointed rock (J). Beneath the sides, scree slopes of coarse material develop (S).

Fig. 46. Steep-sided dry valleys in the Carboniferous Limestone of the Yorkshire Pennines, above Malham, with dry-stone walling. Consider the reasons for the many different angles of slope.

Solution and Karst Scenery

Fig. 48 shows, in more detail, the effects of solution on jointed limestones. Acidic surface water has slowly enlarged surface irregularities in which it remains after storms, so that there are many solution hollows. In these, as in the larger hollows and valleys in Karst country, sufficient impurities from the dissolving limestone remain to form a deep red soil—*terra rossa*. Where such residual soils have accumulated in valleys in Mediterranean limestones, they are frequently the only cultivated parts of an otherwise dry, rocky landscape.

The type of limestone and the nature of its jointing influence the local topography, and may account for the presence or absence of Karst features. In England there are marked differences in scenery on the Jurassic limestones of the Cotswolds compared with the Karst features of the older Carboniferous mountain limestones of the Pennines (Fig. 46) and of the Mendips. Those seen in Fig. 48 are younger than either of these. They show the effects of exposure to maritime influences and winter rains—though much of the solution probably occurred under the climatic conditions of earlier times.

Fig. 48. A Karst surface near the north coast of Malta. Weaknesses along bedding planes and joints have been widened by solution to create the broken limestone 'pavements'. Red soils fill the solution hollows and support grasses and drought-resistant plants, like the aloes.

27

Heated Ground Water in Volcanic Regions

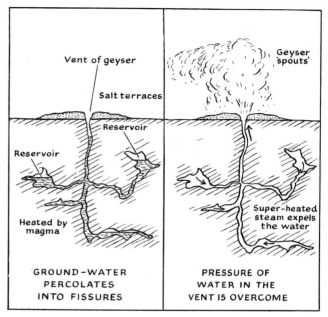

Fig. 50.

Ground water percolates into fissures and reservoirs beneath the surface; so that in volcanic regions, where the rock temperatures are high, the temperature of such ground water rises to near the boiling point (affected by the pressure of the water column above it).

Dissolved gases bubble up, and at intervals froth out at the surface through the water column, releasing pressure so rapidly that a great fount of hot water and steam is forced out, often shooting hundreds of feet into the air. The time taken for this cycle of water accumulation, heating, and spouting is usually fairly constant.

Fig. 49. A geyser in action amid the igneous rocks of the Volcanic Plateau of the North Island of New Zealand. The rocks around are covered with salts crystallised out from the cooling water.

Earth Pillars

The pages which follow show how the force of falling and running water may transform the surface features. Fig. 51 underlines this statement and shows the effects of many such processes (described on the pages indicated). Make a sketch-map of this landscape and mark on it:

1. The earth pillars and their cap rocks (p. 33).
2. Major slips on the hillsides.
3. Gulleying at various places on the valley sides (p. 38).
4. Where flowing water has, in places, actively eroded the lower slopes above the valley bottom (p. 38).

Elsewhere, the effects of ice action are to be seen. Notice:

5. Significant breaks of slope on the sides of the main, glaciated Rhône Valley (p. 88).
6. The nature of the glacial deposits which have been so heavily eroded in the Val d'Herens.

With reference to the pages mentioned, consider how the present landscape, as seen in Fig. 51, has evolved, and the actions which have affected it in glacial and post-glacial times.

Fig. 51. Buttresses of boulder clay have been formed in the Val d'Herens, from which the earth pillars have developed, beneath the capping boulders. Beyond are the Rhône Valley and the Bernese Oberland.

The Smooth Profiles of the Chalk

Fig. 52. A large farm on the Sussex Downs, chiefly devoted to pastoral farming. The view is from part of a long dry valley, which winds for miles through the Downs and is now a main artery of communication.

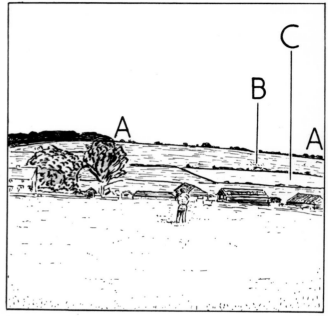

Fig. 53.

The texture of this soft limestone is very different from that of the mountain limestone seen in Fig. 46. Here the scenery lacks the dramatic effects, the abrupt changes of slope and steep-sided valleys of the countryside composed mainly of mountain limestone blocks. The porous chalk absorbs much of the rainfall into the mass of the rock, and there is little surface run-off.

Notice the smoothness of the skyline AA. Scars on the foreslope show that solution hollows and chalk slips can occur, as at B. The arable land (C) shows both the whiteness of the chalky soil and the reddish hues seen in soils derived from chemically basic rocks (like limestone), where iron salts tend to be retained at the surface (Fig. 10).

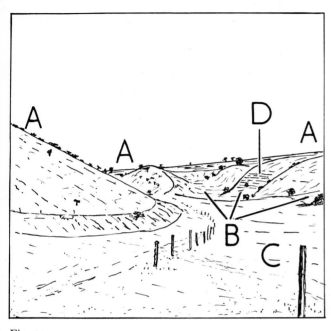

Fig. 54.

Fig. 55. A dry valley in the chalk on the western edge of Salisbury Plain, near Lavington, and close to the moist Vale of Pewsey and the Wiltshire Avon.

Many of the present valleys in chalk country were cut at a time when the water-table was permanently high, and obviously well above the present average levels—probably when the sub-soil was frozen and water from ice-melt flowed freely over this periglacial countryside (p. 104).

Notice the smooth contours (A); the dry drainage channels on the slope (B); and also the soil movements indicated by the 'terracettes' at D.

There had, in fact, been recent heavy rainfall, and water was high in the nearby River Avon. But, despite this, the main valley (C) remained completely dry.

River Systems

Fig. 56A. A well marked *watershed* or *divide*, which separates the tributaries of the two principal rivers A and B. As the streams eat back into, and perhaps through, the ridge the position of the watershed may change (see p. 44).

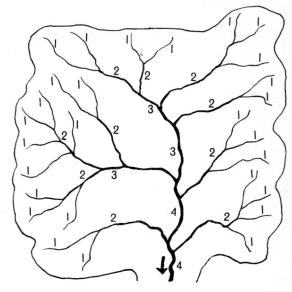

Fig. 56B. The drainage network of a river, and the order of magnitude of its many tributaries.

Drainage Patterns

Water running over the land surface is conveyed to the sea through a multitude of channels, some minute, some miles in width; all may be part of a main *river system*, as in Fig. 56B.

Although we tend to know the names of the major channels (i.e. larger rivers), and may discuss their features and their actions on the landscape, it is the less well-known, and the unknown, smaller tributaries which by their very number, and acting as a whole, create, destroy, and modify the existing landforms in a humid climate.

Fig. 56B shows a drainage network of streams. The channels have been given an *order of magnitude*. Two first order streams join to form a second order one; two second order streams form a third; and two third order streams a fourth order one. The enclosing line represents the extent of the tributary system of the fourth order stream—a *watershed* between the tributary streams and those of the neighbouring river systems.

It can be seen that the whole system is made up of small stream basins, each separated by its own watershed from those of the neighbouring streams.

Run-off

After heavy rain the surface water runs down tiny channels, or *rills*, washing into them debris from the hillsides. The density of such drainage channels on the surface varies with the rock type and climate. Most of the tiny streams will cease to flow after a storm: but lower down will be *streams* sustained by water which has soaked into soil, sub-soil, and rocks, which has raised the general water-table, and is finding its way into water courses in sufficient quantity to maintain a permanent flow. The streams in their turn contribute water to the larger channels of a *river* system.

The deepening of each channel means a steeper fall for the smaller tributary above, and an extra incentive for that stream also to erode with more energy. Heavy rainfall scours out the small hillside channels, and allows them to be incised ever deeper into the landscape. So even at the highest parts of a river basin the surface is being actively lowered (Fig. 57).

Erosion by Rainfall Itself

The force of the raindrops themselves may disturb the soil, and in areas of very loosely bedded rock may cause *earth pillars* to develop. These are relics

Run-off from heavy storms enlarges
otherwise dry water-courses (W)

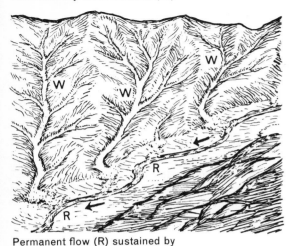

Permanent flow (R) sustained by
ground water

Fig. 57. Tributary channels—temporary and permanent.

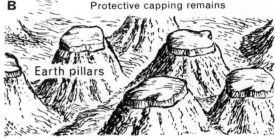

A Boulders protect earth
beneath them

Surface easily eroded

B Protective capping remains

Earth pillars

Fig. 58.

of a drastically eroded surface which have survived because of the protection afforded by a capping boulder (Figs. 51 and 58). More usually the rain acts on slopes unprotected by vegetation by loosening the soil and slowly shifting it downhill. Heavy rain may also give rise to 'sheet erosion', where a continuous sheet of storm water washes material along almost level surfaces; sometimes thousands of tiny rills develop on such gentle slopes.

It is stream action which has such great and continuing effects on the landscape; these activities include the processes of erosion, transportation, and deposition of the eroded material.

Stream Erosion

The force of the water in the stream can itself erode rocks of loose material, such as a poorly con-solidated sandstone. But even hard rocks can be worn away fairly rapidly by the action of *corrasion*, whereby the small boulders and pebbles carried along by the stream act as 'tools of erosion' and abrade the rocks as they strike or grind against the sides and floor of a valley. Fig. 75 shows how the long-continued spiralling action of water over a stream bed has caused pebbles to swirl round and round, and cut or flute hard rock into smoothed channels or deep *potholes*.

The force of the stream itself depends partly on the water available and partly on the distance the stream must drop to reach *base-level*, that is the level of the river, lake, or sea into which it flows. In the case of the main river of the system this will be the sea, and the base-level is that below which erosion is unable to proceed. Streams high up in the system, well above their base-level have the energy to deepen their channel rapidly, with the aid of the rocks and pebbles they transport (their *load*). In time, the water-borne rocks break each other down by *attrition*, and the particles of the load become smaller and smaller; so that many of the 'more mature' rivers, lower in the system, carry a large, muddy load of small silt or clay particles.

Deposition

When the gradient down which the water flows decreases, the stream, no longer able to transport all its load, begins to deposit it; it generally drops the largest calibre first and carries along much of the very fine material even when its energy is greatly reduced. Sometimes the gradient decreases abruptly and much material is suddenly deposited.

The Movement of Water Through Rocks

During an exceptionally wet April, when late snow had just melted on Exmoor, the river Aller, which flows into Porlock Bay, could not contain the run-off and extensive flooding took place.

Figs. 59-61 show how the flood waters were ponded back by the very high pebble ridge. Due to this unusual water-level, much of the flood water seeped through the retaining ridge, and effectively produced a high-water table within the ridge itself. The result was a line of springs along the sea-ward slope. From there great volumes of water poured across the shingle, forming valleys, which in some cases coalesced.

Fig. 59. The high barrier beach which has been built up by the sea about Porlock Bay in west Somerset, here seen where it adjoins a spur of Exmoor, Hurlstone Point. To the right are floods from the Aller Valley. (See also p. 143).

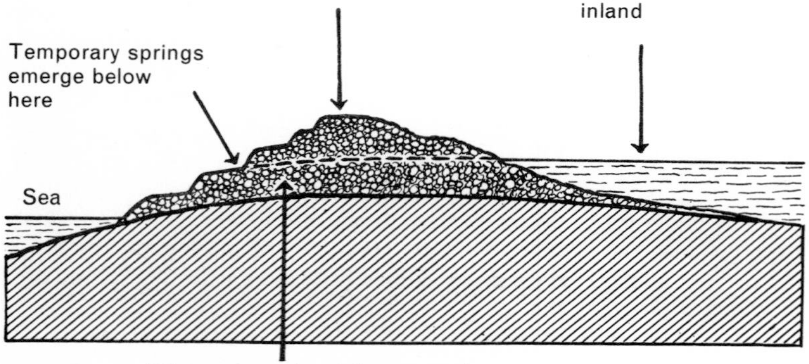

Pebble ridges thrown up during high seas

Exceptionally high flood water inland

Temporary springs emerge below here

Sea

Water seeps through saturated zone

Fig. 60. Diagrammatic section of the Ridge.

Spring Water and the Headward Erosion of a Valley

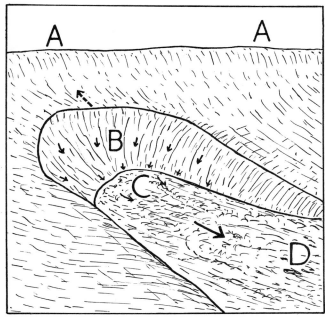

Fig. 61. Headward erosion.

In Fig. 62 water emerges as a strong spring (C), and flows swiftly down the pebbles (D) to a base-level thirty feet or more below. The swirling waters displace and transport pebbles, forming a valley. (Small arrows show pebbles falling.)

At the head of the valley, the pebbles rattle and roar down the steep, undercut face and are carried downstream. In this way the valley head (B) retreats rapidly, and the valley is extended deep into the ridge (broken arrow). In fact, it did not break through the ridge before the flood-level dropped—for the 'hill-top' (AA) is a false crest, being the top of a storm ridge, and the whole beach is wider than appears in the picture (see Fig. 60).

Fig. 62. One of a line of springs which appeared on the pebble ridge at the north-east corner of Porlock Bay, following river flooding inland. A 'speeded-up' example of a valley being extended headward.

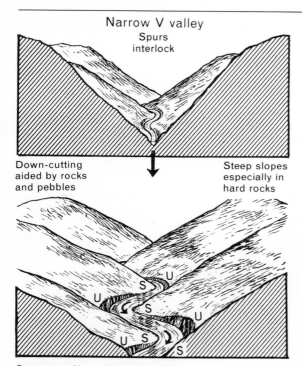

Narrow V valley
Spurs
interlock

Down-cutting
aided by rocks
and pebbles

Steep slopes
especially in
hard rocks

S – spur   U – active undercutting

Fig. 63.

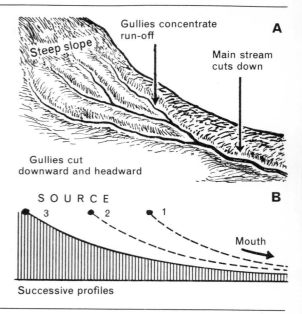

Fig. 64. In A erosion of the valley head is being accelerated. B looks at the valley in profile, from source to mouth, and illustrates how lengthening accompanies deepening.

Steep slope

Gullies concentrate
run-off

A

Main stream
cuts down

Gullies cut
downward and headward

S O U R C E

B

3   2   1

Mouth

Successive profiles

Characteristics of Youthful Rivers

A stream high above its base-level, with plenty of energy, is said to be 'young'. The stream tends to cascade over irregularities and cuts rapidly downwards, so that its valley tends to be 'V'-shaped with steep sides, or gorge-like in resistant rocks. It also undercuts the banks on the outside of its bends, and thus tends to leave the valley slopes as projecting spurs, which, looking upstream, appear to interlock (Figs. 63 and 73). Its main activity, however, is downward erosion.

Fig. 63 shows the valley profile created by a youthful active stream, as described on p. 33. The velocity of water is much greater under flood conditions in such a narrow valley; for at low water, despite the steep gradient, there is much energy lost by friction on the bed and sides. In flood a stream of this kind may transport really large boulders. The lower sketch shows how erosion of the valley sides at the outer parts of the bends, as the river naturally meanders, or swings about obstructions, tends, in time, to produce interlocking valley spurs.

The valley sides are usually much steeper when the rocks are hard and resistant, and the valley narrower. The undercutting of soft rocks tends to lead to slumping of the sides and the valley is widened more easily.

The downward erosion of a river bed is often accompanied by headward erosion at the head of the valley. In young streams, the long profile of the valley is strongly concave (Fig. 64). Rills and gullies concentrate water at the head of the stream channel. This causes strong down-cutting, and with the steepening of the slopes parts of the valley head may slump forward, causing the hillside to recede. Emergent springs tend to cause the same effect (p. 35), so that the head of the valley retreats and the valley is thus lengthened. In some cases, this may cause, in time, a ridge or watershed to be breached by headward erosion (Fig. 78).

In Fig. 64 B we see that as the stream cuts downwards from the position of its bed shown in Profile 1, it lessens its gradient; and as the head of the valley is extended from position 1 to 2, to 3, the valley itself is lengthened.

In nature, the bed of a youthful stream is unlikely to have such a smooth profile, but responds rather to the irregularities of the rocks over which

Changes of Energy

STRAIGHT CHANNEL

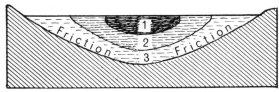

Rate of flow

1 – Fastest 2 – Less fast 3 – Slowest

Fig. 65A. Rates of flow in various parts of a stream channel.

BEND

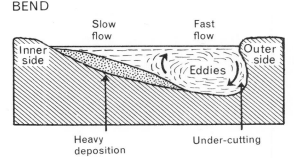

Fig. 65B. Erosion and deposition within the bend of a channel.

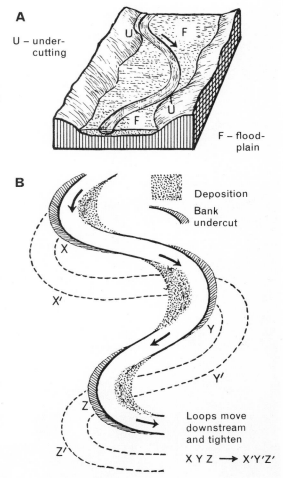

Fig. 66. Notice how in B the bends migrate from XYZ to X′Y′Z′.

it flows. In time, however, it tends to remove obstructions and to even out its bed.

The Mature Stage

In the middle reaches of most rivers the gradient has become less, and, here, where the tributaries add both to the volume of water and the load of material transported, the valley is said to show features typical of a *mature* stage.

The flow of river water in a straight channel is not greatly retarded in the middle, but, as one might expect, is held back by friction near the bed and sides. This is shown diagrammatically in Fig. 65A.

The now broader river tends to deposit some of its load, which may now be of gravel, sand, or fine silt, at the sides and on the bed of the river. Depending on how far it is above base-level, the river will still tend to cut downwards, strongly or

otherwise. There is often, therefore, a delicate balance between erosion and deposition, varying also with low-water or flood periods.

In the now wider valley the river swings, or *meanders*, from side to side. The river loops tend to migrate downstream, and thus act both to straighten and widen the valley (Fig. 66).

At the outside of each bend where the current is fastest, eddying occurs, and the banks are under-cut (Fig. 65B). On the inside of the bend there is much deposition of gravelly material in the slack water. Both processes tend to cause the main channel to move across the valley.

Undercutting takes place strongly on the down-stream side of the outer part of the bend, so that any remaining spurs are gradually removed, and the valley widened. The loops of the river tend to move downstream for these same reasons, as shown in Fig. 66B.

Surface Run-off and Youthful Features

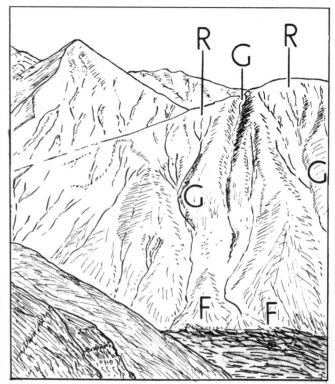

Fig. 68.

These Alpine slopes are too steep to maintain a permanent flow of water; and yet, at times of heavy rainfall or snow-melt, the many steep-sided channels, carved by water erosion into the rocky slopes, carry down water and eroded material towards lower systems of drainage. Storm waters have created rills (R) and steep-sided gullies (G). Most of the material worn from these channels is deposited at the chief break of slope, where alluvial fans (F) are created.

Fig. 67. Run-off channels on an Alpine mountain face.

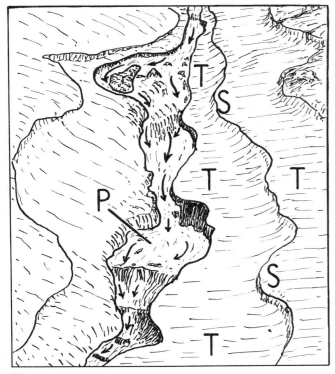

Fig. 69.

It is not essential to follow the upper courses of large and well-known rivers in order to observe many of the typical features of youthful streams. A small water-channel can often illustrate the behaviour of larger streams.

Fig. 70 shows a tiny stream in its torrent stage, actively eroding the moorland hillside. On the ground, as shown diagrammatically by Fig. 69, it is obvious that at times when much water is carried by the channel the stream floods over the lower terrace T, and creates spurs like S, to the left of its course. There is evidence of a higher terrace T. Notice the plunge pool (P) being deepened, below the series of falls and rapids.

Fig. 70. An Exmoor stream, amid a litter of old bracken.

The Flood-Plain

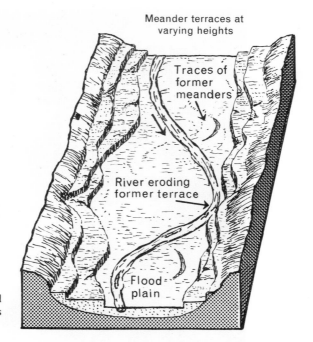

Meander terraces at
varying heights

Traces of
former
meanders

River eroding
former terrace

Flood
plain

Fig. 71. Parts of former flood-plains are being removed by the river, and relics of these still stand at various heights on both sides of the valley.

Features of the Flood-Plain

In times of flood, the now mature river may overflow its banks and carry the suspended particles across the wide valley. These materials are thus deposited and cover the *flood-plain* with fine silt and clay which, because of the mixture of minerals in them, are likely, if well-drained, to prove fertile for vegetation and the growth of crops.

The gravelly deposits which accumulate in the stretches of slack water along the inner bends of the meanders are also left as the channel migrates across its valley, and help to build up the flood-plain. These thick gravel deposits are sometimes

revealed in terraces which are left stranded above the present river level—flat, well-drained ledges which, being now above the flood level, but perhaps covered with finer material in the past, are often valuable settlement sites.

Meander Terraces

Traces of old meanders and cut-off loops are often visible, and may at times carry water.
These are built from alluvial materials, as just described. The term *alluvium* refers to any material which has been transported by water and then deposited, and includes coarse gravels as well as fine sands and clays.

A river in a mature valley erodes laterally and vertically, and also deposits some of its load. Should a balance be achieved between the rate of deposition and the rate of vertical erosion, so that neither process dominates, and if the gradient at which the river flows is a stable one, then the river is said to be 'at grade'. However, many mature rivers with well-formed flood-plains are still cutting downwards. In time, the loops of the meanders move downstream and across the valley, though parts of the flood-plain remain un-eroded for long periods. Elsewhere the valley is being widened and the river bed also lowered.

When, ultimately, loops of the river from up-

40

A

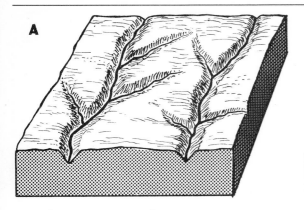

Young streams rapidly
dissect the plateau.
Divides are accentuated
and become hill masses.

B

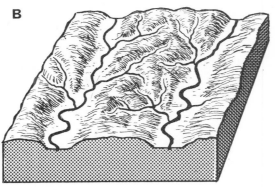

Mature valleys develop.
Their tributaries flow
from distinct hilly
interfluves.

C

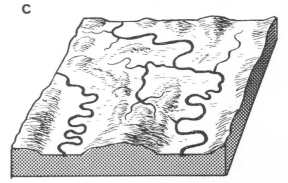

Valleys have been widened.
Flood plains are separated
by low divides. River
capture has occurred.
Residual hills stand out.

Fig. 72. Following the uplift shown in A, a cycle of erosion takes place, with tributary streams developing and becoming active in eroding the landscape: hence the mature scenery of B, with the well-defined hills and valleys. In time, aided by weathering and other processes of denudation (removal of surface features), these too disappear and the landscape again tends to become featureless (C). In nature, of course, such a cycle may be interrupted by further relative changes of land/sea level, by climatic changes, etc. It must also be emphasised that physical processes may bring about conditions of balance, or equilibrium, in any landscape, and interrupt the so-called 'cycle'—whose 'stages' are by no means inevitable.

---

stream work their way back across the valley towards the long abandoned parts of the flood-plain, these loops will be at a lower level. By cutting sideways they may remove much of the old deposits; but nevertheless some usually remains at its original height, and stands out as a *terrace* above the new plain level.

Traces of terraces at varying heights remain along the valley sides. They are not 'paired' by height on either side of the valley, as are terraces abandoned by a river down-cutting in response to a fall in sea-level or a relatively rapid uplift of the land surface (p. 61).

Valleys and the Landscape

We can now see more fully the effects of the lowering of the bed of the main river in consequence of the downward erosion towards sea-level. The many tributaries for which the river itself is the local base-level must tend to become more active, and in this way a whole landscape may be affected.

Stages in the development of a drainage system are shown, in an idealised form, in Fig. 72. Youthful streams are seen, in A, cutting into an uplifted plain surface: the landscape itself is featureless (perhaps worn down long ago, before uplift). Gradually a mature landscape develops, as

seen in B. But the erosion continues until, in C, only the residual hills of an 'old' surface remain (hills called *monadnocks*).

The Meaning of Age

All of this emphasises that 'youth', 'maturity', and 'old age' are terms which do not necessarily describe both the river valleys and the surrounding landscape at a particular time. Youthful valleys may develop in an almost featureless landscape; later both may show mature features but not necessarily. It is essential, therefore, to use terms of 'age' with particular care.

Youthful Features

Fig. 73. An Alpine river in its youthful stage; a picture which clearly shows the interlocking, or overlapping, spurs, typical of the valleys formed by such streams.

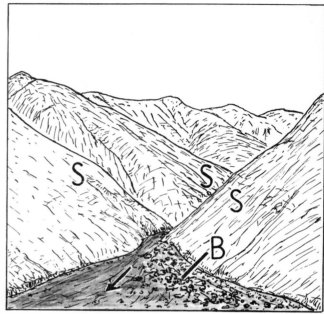

Fig. 74.

At this stage rivers are actively cutting downwards, especially in flood conditions. Here the streams are fed by snow-melt as well as by rainfall, and at times of high water the boulders B, seen on the stream bed, are used by the torrent as powerful 'tools of erosion'; see Fig. 75.

The bottom of the valley is hardly wider than the stream channel. The load carried is small at this stage: thus much energy is available for the erosion of the bed and, where the current is deflected, of the outside of the bends.

River Abrasion and Pot-holes

The stream shown in Fig. 75 flows in a narrow channel of hard rock, down a steep gradient, and so becomes highly turbulent as the water level rises.

These conditions favour the formation of potholes; for eddies in the water tend to swirl pebbles and small particles in spiral paths, and so drill holes in the bedrock, by abrasion.

Apart from the fluted channels and almost circular potholes, the smoothness of these hard rocks is also the result of abrasion. In many streams of this type the eddying effect is sufficient to loosen jointed rocks and lift away quite large blocks; this may, in fact, be the cause of some of the irregularities in the bed of the stream.

This particular Mediterranean stream carries little water during the summer, but fills rapidly, though intermittently, during the winter months. Its deep valley was probably formed mainly during an earlier, wetter period.

Fig. 75. The bed of a tributary of the Rio Verde, in southern Spain, at low water.

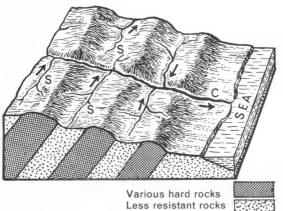

Various hard rocks

Less resistant rocks

Fig. 76. Development of trellised drainage.

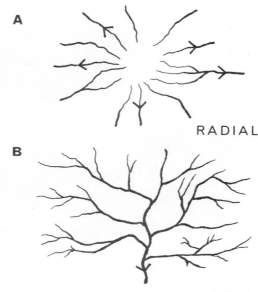

A

RADIAL

B

DENDRITIC

C

TRELLISED

Fig. 77. Patterns of drainage influenced by structure—strongly in A and C, weakly in B.

River Patterns

The river systems tend to acquire patterns in response to the general structure of the landscape and to various outstanding features of that landscape. Among the more typical patterns are: *radial* drainage, as tends to develop on domes or volcanic cones (C in Fig. 186); *dendritic* forms of drainage, with streams like the veins of a leaf, usually where there is no strong structural influence; *trellised* drainage, which is common where parallel outcrops of different rocks lie almost at right angles to the overall slope, down which the dominant river flows; this occurs in the English scarplands, where the escarpments of the more resistant rocks alternate with vales formed on weaker sands and clays. Fig. 76 shows how a trellised drainage pattern develops on a surface where tilt and uplift have produced a number of parallel scarps. The main streams which flow to the sea in response to the seaward slope of the uplifted surface are called

consequent streams (C). The others which have, later, developed along the vales, and do not follow the initial slope, are the *subsequent* streams (S).

River Capture

A subsequent stream may be able to erode a deep valley in the weaker rocks, and also to extend backwards the head of its valley (p. 36) until it breaches a watershed and takes water from another river system. It thus effects a *river capture*. A 'wind gap' (with no stream flowing through it) is left at the *elbow of capture*. Below this the river is left deprived of much of its tributary water, and is therefore unable to cut downwards so effectively.

By contrast, the river which receives additional water is able to erode more powerfully, so that all parts of its system receive an extra incentive to cut down. Hence the whole extended river system now erodes the landscape more effectively.

It is often the case that, following a series of captures affecting several parallel streams, the

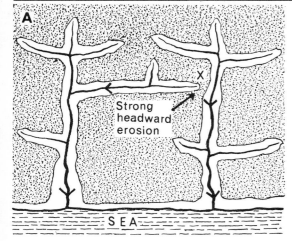

A

Strong headward erosion

X

S E A

B

X

Elbow of capture

Wind gap

S E A

Fig. 78. In A a left-bank tributary is able to erode strongly and eats backwards towards X, at which point the watershed is breached. In B the streams of the enlarged system are seen to be more active and acquire well-defined tributaries.

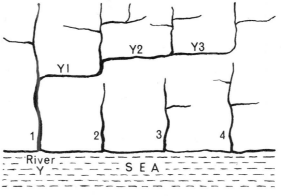

Y1   Y2   Y3

1   2   3   4

River Y   S E A

Consequent courses 1 – 4
Subsequent courses Y1, Y2, Y3

Fig. 79. The river Y. Former subsequents, through capture, make up the greater part of its course.

longest stretches of a river, like Y in Fig. 79, are the courses of the former subsequent streams, which, overall, comprise most of its length.

Superimposed Patterns

In some cases a river flows across a landscape with an apparent disregard for the local structure. This may be because the pattern of drainage was initiated on a surface which overlay the present one. As erosional processes removed the surface above, so the pattern of the rivers became incised in the very different rocks beneath.

Fig. 80 shows how such a river system develops on a more or less uniform surface (A). In B the original surface has long since been removed, but the drainage pattern is recognisably the same, even though the rivers are breaching the rocks beneath. In time, of course, this basic pattern will be modified as new tributaries develop along the valleys of weaker rocks, as hinted at in B.

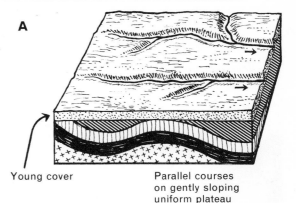

A

Young cover

Parallel courses on gently sloping uniform plateau

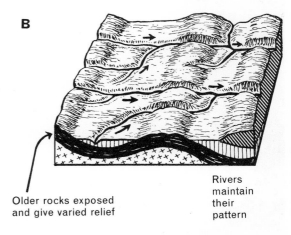

B

Older rocks exposed and give varied relief

Rivers maintain their pattern

Fig. 80. The young cover-rocks in A act as a 'template' which, when removed, as at B, are seen to have guided the incision into the later landscape.

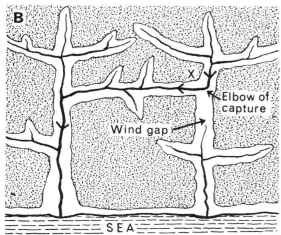

Deposition in the Stream Channels

In mountain regions rivers may acquire a load of heavy material; much of this is later deposited where the gradient lessens, perhaps where it begins to cross an adjacent lowland, or flows into a flat-floored, broad valley of glacial origin. Rivers which have their sources in glaciers are apt to carry much coarse material and deposit it in their main water channels.

The main flow, within these particular channels in the river bed, may therefore be diverted to others, which in turn may fill up with the load they transport. In this way midstream islands of gravel build up and become exposed, and there may, perhaps, be braiding (p. 48) with continually shifting channels.

The amount of water carried by a river course like that in Fig. 81 varies considerably. Rapid run-off from mountains during a rainy period, or sudden snow-melt, can raise the level and allow the river to transport a heavy load: conversely, a fall in level may cause much deposition. The stranded lines of boulders near the banks show what size of material the river may shift during flood periods.

Fig. 81. The River Traun, in Austria, shows the mid-stream gravel banks which may accumulate in low, slack-water conditions, but shift as the volume of water increases.

Deposition and Erosion by a Mature River

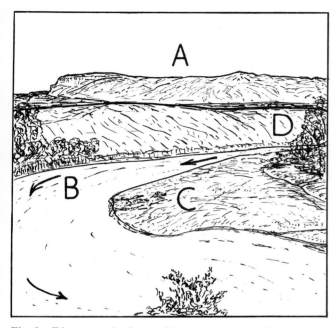

Fig. 82. Diagrammatic view—with tree-cover reduced.

Fig. 83. The River Calore in south-western Italy crosses part of the plain which lies between the faulted limestone hills (A) and the Gulf of Salerno. Cattle lie on the massive gravel bank on the inside of the bend.

Deposition takes place in the slacker water on the inside of the bend, and here a large sloping bank of sand and gravel (C) has accumulated. The river has cut into the soft, relatively recent deposits of the plain (D), so that the slip-off slope (C) lies in the form of a terrace, a thick bank of gravel.

From this bank the deposits continue to build out and narrow the channel, so that the river, flowing swiftly on the outside of the bend, cuts into the far bank (B) and widens the channel on this side. This and other loops, therefore, are tending to incise themselves and also migrate across the plain.

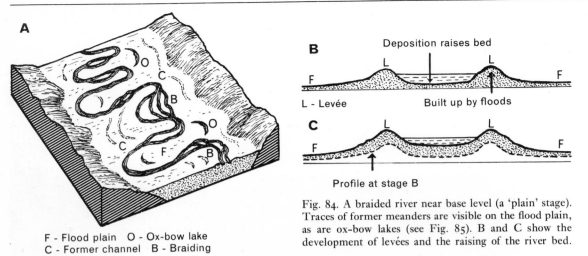

F - Flood plain   O - Ox-bow lake
C - Former channel   B - Braiding

B Deposition raises bed

F   L   L   F

L - Levée   Built up by floods

C

F   L   L   F

Profile at stage B

Fig. 84. A braided river near base level (a 'plain' stage). Traces of former meanders are visible on the flood plain, as are ox-bow lakes (see Fig. 85). B and C show the development of levées and the raising of the river bed.

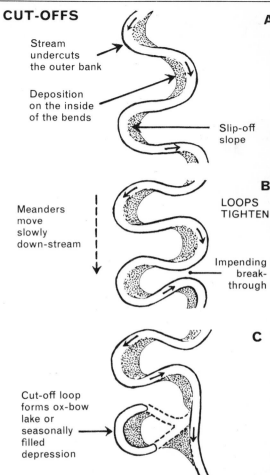

CUT-OFFS   **A**

Stream undercuts the outer bank

Deposition on the inside of the bends

Slip-off slope

B

Meanders move slowly down-stream

LOOPS TIGHTEN

Impending break-through

C

Cut-off loop forms ox-bow lake or seasonally filled depression

Fig. 85. Stages in the development of a cut-off loop.

The Plain Stage

As the river profile flattens out and the river is not far above base-level (for main rivers, the sea) deposition is the most important process. The river tends to meander over a broad, almost level valley, and in flood the waters spread far from the main channel, so that alluvial deposits are left; these build up over the flood-plain, the coarsest dropped first, the finest widely distributed.

The excess load within the main channel is deposited where the flow is slackest—at the sides and along the bed of the river. Gravelly mounds cause the stream to divide and redivide like braided rope—the effect is known, in fact, as *braiding*. Sand and gravel fill in the channels and cause streams to change their course (Fig. 84 A).

In flood, the material dropped is also greatest near the river sides. As the flood water overspills, alluvial deposits so build up that they form raised banks, parallel with the stream and higher than the

adjacent flood-plain (Fig. 84). These banks are natural *levées*. As the river bed is built up annually, so the river, at high water, is caused to flood over the levées, and in each succeeding year the pattern is repeated. In time the river comes to flow, as do the great Mississippi and Hwang Ho, high above the adjacent flood-plain. Under these conditions, it is obvious that disastrous flooding may occur from time to time.

Fig. 85 shows that as river meanders move down-stream (p. 37) the loops become tighter and bends advance as the outer banks are eroded away. Deposition continues on the inside, until, by a combination of these processes, some loops are cut off. They are visible as crescent-shaped depressions, or, when water-filled, as *ox-bow lakes*.

These flood-plain features may be seen where the stream gradient is slight, far from the sea. A river, far inland, may flow to a lake through a flat flood-plain and construct a delta.

48

Deposition

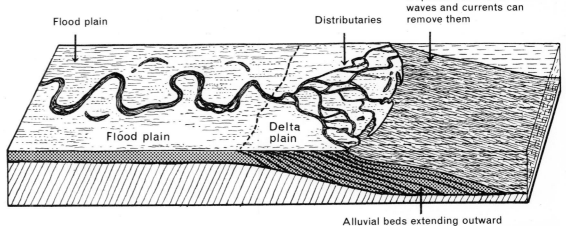

Fig. 86. The formation of a delta.

The flood-plain of a river in its old age is thus usually characterised by a maze of old abandoned loops and former river channels, lying alongside the present ones. Like the cut-off meanders, they may bear water during a wet period, when the water-table is particularly high, and give rise to swampy stretches on either side of the river.

The levées along the lower course may prevent tributary streams which are wandering across the flood-plain from joining the main river, so that they may flow for mile after mile parallel to the principal channels before joining the main flow. These are sometimes called Yazoo rivers, after a long river of this type in the lower Mississippi basin.

It should be remembered that not all such plains are necessarily near the sea, but may be found, for instance, upriver of a lake, whose surface is the base level for part of a river course: another reason why terms like 'old age' are often misleading.

Delta Formation

At the mouth of a river, the outflow of water may carry with it such a load of sediment that the rate at which it is deposited may exceed the rate at which waves or currents can remove it.

The checks in the rate of flow of the river water as it enters a lake or sea causes rapid deposition of part of the load; this is helped by salt water, which acts to cause tiny alluvial particles to form larger clusters and so sink more easily.

The lake bottom, or a shallow sea-floor or shelf, will therefore receive a mass of sediment, which accumulates until it builds up to the level of the flood-plain itself. The river is thus caused to create and follow channels through this new mass of alluvial deposits.

Fig. 86 shows how the sediments build up, like underwater embankments—the coarser material being dropped first, and the finer carried further out to accumulate more slowly on the sea floor.

The Mature River: A Closer Balance
Between Erosion and Deposition

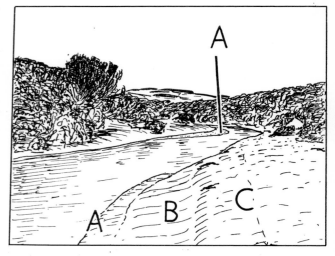

Fig. 88.

Here the broad river loops gently through a well-defined valley. Though apparently contained within its banks, the volume of water and the load carried by the stream can greatly, and rapidly increase at times of heavy run-off from the hills. Deposition of some of the load is seen here, where the gravelly slip-off slope builds outwards on the inside of the bend at A.

The river, however, has long been cutting downwards, and continues to do so; and the lower of the terraces, in the foreground, once built up in the same manner as at A, shows a similar gravelly composition. In this stage neither erosion not deposition necessarily predominate, and the face of the higher terrace, C, displays the effects of erosion caused during exceptionally high floods.

Fig. 87. A mature valley, with the river flowing entrenched in the beautiful Southern Uplands of Scotland: a scene which is typical of the middle valleys of the Tweed and its tributaries.

Flood Plains of the Middle Valley

Though meandering in tight loops, this small, fast-flowing river is still actively engaged in widening its valley.

In the foreground it is undercutting the lower slope of the near valley side; while in the distance it is eating into the lower part of the wooded spur on the far side of the valley. It is, in fact, so active that a mile or so further downstream, near Cleeve Abbey, it has been confined by man into a narrow, walled channel, in order to prevent it further undermining the adjacent road.

Still further downstream, near Watchet, during high water the Washford river floods a wide expanse of farmland, where, only a mile or so from the sea, it has entered into its lower, plain stage.

In this picture, it is seen slightly incised in its flood-plain, and the flat water-meadows are flooded less seldom. In this middle part of the course, the typical slip-off slope of the deposits on the inside of the river bend can just be seen through the trees in the foreground, part of the first meander downstream.

Fig. 89. The flood-plain of the small Washford River which flows from the Brendon Hills in West Somerset, carrying a heavy load of fine red particles and coarser gravel. Here it meanders in slightly incised loops through the flat meadows.

Deposition

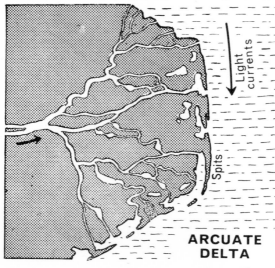

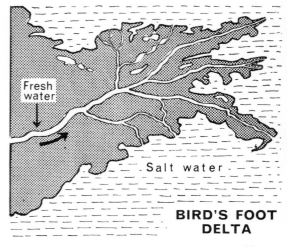

Fig. 90.

Fig. 91.

Delta Shapes

In many deltas the sediments build out into a fan shape, settling in a broad and expanding arc about the mouth of the river. It is from this *arcuate*, or *fan*, shape, resembling the Greek letter delta (△), that the term derives.

As alluvium blocks the river mouth, the main stream is forced to split up into a large number of separate channels, or *distributaries*, which carry the water and alluvium further into the sea or lake. The channels themselves shift about as their beds become silted, so that traces of old channels and various types of cut-off lakes are included in the delta (Fig. 90).

Currents may form spits (p. 140) along the foreshore of the delta as material is drifted across the outer edge of the deposits, and lagoons become ponded up behind the blocking debris.

In other cases, streams of fresh water may carry

sediment a long way forward as a muddy flow. This is especially the case where the river water is markedly less dense than the water into which it flows. Deposits accumulate in quantity along the sides of these channels, and low levées may even be built up. Hence there tends to be a finger-like growth, with some extensions growing more quickly than others.

This type of deposition creates a *bird's foot delta*. The Mississippi delta is a well-defined example of this kind, whereas the Nile delta is a clear example of the arcuate type. All have minor distributaries, and may show spit and lagoon formation.

Deltaic deposits may become immensely thick, and, if the earth's crust sags locally under such weight, even more sediment may then accumulate. It must be remembered, however, that waves and currents may remove much material and that currents may become more effective as the delta expands, and so limit further growth.

As the delta extends seawards, the earlier deposits, now well inland, tend to become covered first with swamp vegetation, and then, as they become more consolidated, develop more typical land types of vegetation; so that, ultimately they become firm extensions of the land area.

Lakes and Their History
Origins

Various types of lake are mentioned in other sections of this book, and nearly every kind of geological process can give rise to, or involve, lake formation. Some of them are associated with:
Structural forms: lakes in crustal depressions.
Faulting: rift valley lakes.
Vulcanicity: crater lakes; lava-blocked lakes.
Glaciation: corrie lakes; ribbon lakes; or lakes in other scoured hollows; lakes in melt hollows; ice-blocked lakes.

Lakes—Their Temporary Nature

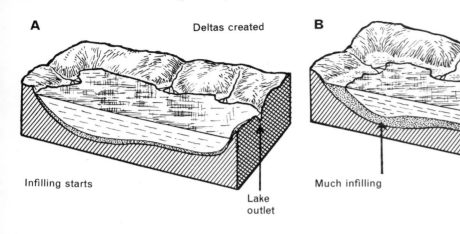

A

Deltas created

Infilling starts

Lake outlet

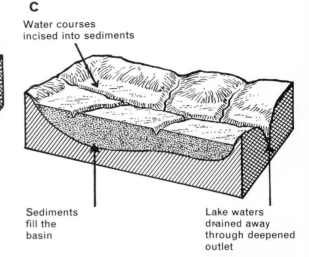

B

Much infilling

Outlet deepened
Lake partly
drained

C

Water courses
incised into sediments

Sediments
fill the
basin

Lake waters
drained away
through deepened
outlet

Fig. 92. The slow extinction of a lake.

Rivers: ox-bow lakes.
Seas: lakes formed behind coastal deposits.
Mass Wasting: lakes behind blocks formed by landslips.

There are in fact countless ways in which hollows may be created so that water may drain in to form a lake, or rise through ground-water sources to occupy the depression. Yet the existence of any lake is apt to hang in the balance, and most are temporary features relative to the geological time-scale.

Lake Filling

A lake in a basin is very often maintained by a surface flow of water; and water carries sediment. This is deposited in the lake. Streams may build up deltas, and these, in time, may merge, gradually filling the basin. Wind may contribute dust or sand particles. Vegetation developing on alluvial deposits may then help to consolidate them, and the former lake becomes a solid feature of the landscape.

Lake Emptying

Changes in climate may cause a lake to shrink by evaporation, or abrupt surface movements may create outlets which drain the lake. But often it is slow erosion by the rivers which flow from the lake which may ultimately drain away its waters.

Fig. 92 shows how each of the processes described above may lead to the extinction of the lake. In A the deltas build out into waters which have an outlet through the river course at the other end of the lake. Of course, there may also be considerable loss of water by evaporation. In B, as the deltas coalesce, the river also cuts a deeper channel, so that the lake is more effectively drained. As the lake shrinks and vanishes (C) the sediments are exposed over the whole area and are, in their turn, eroded by surface streams.

Deltaic Deposits

For large amounts of material to be deposited by flowing water in a particular locality, the stream must obviously carry a large load. Many of the hillsides in Greece continue to suffer severe erosion as the result of many centuries of deforestation and of grazing, especially by goats; this is aggravated by the seasonal contrasts in climatic conditions, whereby sudden storms after lengthy drought cause the removal of dry, loose surface material by rapid run-off.

A change in the gradient of the stream bed, sufficient to check the flow, causes deposition of the heavier material in torrent and stream courses on the way to the coast; but streams entering the coastal plains still carry a load of fine particles, and build up flats of the type seen in Fig. 93.

Notice the wandering channels carrying the water through the alluvial barrier. They behave like any other stream, and here the deposition on the inside of the near bend, with its convex slope, and the undercut bank on the outer side are clearly visible. As a result, channels fill on the inside and flow more strongly on the outside, so that they are forever shifting within the delta. Just to the right of the picture, the arms of a perfect small ox-bow lake can be seen.

Fig. 93. Part of a deltaic lowland in eastern Greece, where many flat coastal plains are built up of thick alluvial deposits which have become consolidated. Here, the vegetation cover is as yet slight, and distributary channels are shifting.

The Delta

The East and West Lyn rivers flow through deep valleys cut into the impervious sandstones of the north-western part of Exmoor. Run-off after storms is rapid; the rivers may then rise tens of feet in their narrow channels, and carry pebbles, rocks, and great boulders down their courses. In the summer of 1952, over nine inches of rain fell on the moors within 24 hours, and onto waterlogged ground. The West Lyn with huge boulders and trees torn from the narrow valley cut a new channel through part of Lynmouth, demolishing roads, bridges, and houses.

Fig. 94 shows the common delta of these rivers and, not surprisingly, much of the material deposited is coarse and bouldery. Nevertheless, this is a true fan-shaped delta, with particles of all sizes. Small lakes, or lagoons, cut off by the deposits, can be seen within the nearer half of the delta, towards which currents drift a greater proportion of the material.

The river maintains a channel through the deposits, and, although this was formerly much braided, the channelling of the flow, and construction made from the point of view of safety, have tended to cause deposition further out.

Fig. 94. At Lynmouth, a fan-shaped delta extends outward into the Bristol Channel, built by the load carried by the East and West Lyn rivers. These deeply incised rivers drain much of the western plateau of Exmoor, which here drops steeply to the sea.

The River in its Plain Stage

In the distance are the eastern foothills of the Southern Alps of New Zealand, whose morainic deposits and easily eroded sandstones provide the rivers with a heavy load. The plains themselves bear a great thickness of loose glacial outwash. The picture well illustrates the winding and braided course of a river in its plain stage, where deposition of sands and gravels are causing the channels to fill and shift, as the slip-off slopes extend into the stream and the flow is deflected. Traces of former channels and old cut-offs can be seen on the wide flood-plain, and even on land which is now fairly well consolidated, like that near the planted forest, to the right. Trees on the plain also reveal the line of former watercourses. (The more regular lines of trees in the background are much-needed windbreaks of introduced, quick-growing pines: these help to protect the arable land from the drying effect of the winds of Föhn origin, which descend from the mountains to the west).

Fig. 95. The River Hurunui, like the others which flow from the Southern Alps of New Zealand across the Canterbury Plains, acquires a very heavy load in its upper reaches, and deposits much of it on its way to the sea. On the right is the Balmoral State Forest.

River Terraces

Otago, in the south of the South Island of New Zealand, has suffered much faulting and earth movements, which have produced landscapes of tilted blocks alternating with basins partly infilled with sediments. Rivers cross the basins and eat into the sediments. Earth movements have resulted in changes of level which are reflected in the profiles of the river valleys.

It is instructive to make a simple sketch of the physical features seen in Fig. 96 and to mark on it:
1. Obvious breaks of slope.
2. The level upper surfaces of the terraces which have been left on either side of the river.
3. The areas of deposition within the river course, and the relatively clear channels between.

Consider the reasons for the location of the level surfaces and of the steep slopes beneath each; and also why the river, which now flows incised in a fairly narrow channel in the main valley, obviously carries and deposits so much alluvial material.

Fig. 96. The Lower Shotover Bridge across the Shotover River, near Queenstown, Otago, in the South Island of New Zealand. The view is from Speargrass Flat, one of the many superb examples of river terraces to be seen in the picture.

The Formation of Terraces

Just as studies of the action of running water may be made with the help of a sand-filled 'wave-tank', so observation of water flowing over a sloping beach can reveal many of the processes which occur on a larger scale in wider landscapes, and, of course, take place so much more quickly.

Here a stream of water emerges from the bank of pebbles and has eroded a valley as it flows to the sea. As the tide recedes the base-level falls, and a series of abandoned terraces stand out on either side of the valley; successive flats with under-cut cliffs are left stranded on the inner side of the main channel, while the stream undercuts the terraces on the outer side.

As the base-level is being lowered continuously, it is unusual to find paired terraces (p. 46) beside this kind of beach channel.

Fig. 97. Water draining from a shingle bank demonstrates processes of terrace formation as it crosses the sloping beach on its way to the sea.

River Terraces

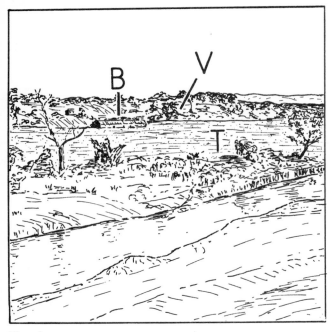

Fig. 98

Fig. 99. In southern Jamaica, near May Pen, tobacco is planted on the alluvial soils of this large, flat terrace; beyond are the long tobacco barns against the valley side.

The Rio Minho now flows slightly incised beneath a former wide flood plain (T). This now forms a terrace of gravelly soils covered by fine, light alluvium. At the far edge of this flood-plain can be seen the slopes of the main valley (V), which rise above the long tobacco barns (B). Tobacco growers make the most of the well-drained but moist soils of the terraces, which lie on both sides of the river.

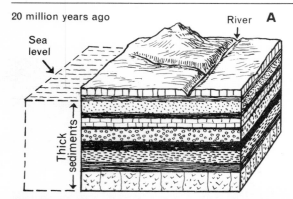

20 million years ago

Sea level

Thick sediments

River **A**

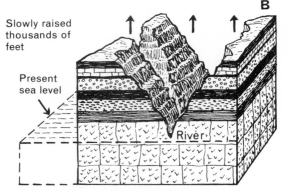

B

Slowly raised thousands of feet

Present sea level

River

Fig. 100. A shows the sea-level millions of years ago, and the thick sediments which had accumulated before that time. A river is cutting into the surface, not far above sea-level. As the mass of sedimentary and base-ment rocks was slowly raised (B), the river created a deep gorge with rock layers of different resistance exposed on its sides.

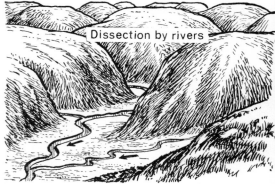

Level summits – an uplifted plain

Dissection by rivers

Valleys eroded by rivers and ice leave mountain blocks

Fig. 101. A mountain landscape evolved by erosion following uplift.

Rejuvenation

We have seen that as a river cuts downward into the landscape, the ultimate level to which the water of the river system drains is sea-level—the base-level for the main stream—and that the various tributary rivers and streams have their local base-level. But the relative levels of land and sea are apt to change. The land regions may slowly emerge, or be heaved upward more rapidly; or the sea-levels may fall the world over, as when large volumes of water are locked in the massive ice-sheets of the near-polar regions, or may rise as the ice-sheets melt.

Among the results of such movements will be the creation of a new base-level for river systems. Thus a nett fall in sea-level will mean that water in rivers, streams, gullies and rills will proceed to

erode with renewed energy. This is illustrated in more detail on p. 61, Fig. 103. Conversely, a rise in base-level will tend to diminish the work done by erosion, and invoke more deposition by rivers and streams.

The lowering of the base-level is said to cause *rejuvenation*—restoring energy to the rivers and more youthful features to the landscape.

We should, however, remember that while the uplift of a surface which is in the last flattened stages of erosion (worn down to what is called a *peneplain*) may produce a level plateau with all the features of old age, yet in this surface the now youthful, rejuvenated rivers create deep, steep-sided gorges. Rivers and the landscape must be considered separately when 'age' is used to describe their stages of development (p. 41).

In many cases, while uplift has proceeded, an

existing river has managed to maintain its course by deepening its valley. Such rivers may form deep gorges, like parts of the Colorado River and its tributaries on the uplifted inter-montane regions west of the Rocky Mountains in the USA. Dry climatic conditions tend to preserve the steepness of the valley sides.

Fairly rapid rejuvenation may cause even tightly meandering rivers to incise their courses—so that the meanders become deeply entrenched in the landscape. Such a rejuvenated river, maintaining its course within the confines of a gorge, is known as an *antecedent* river.

In various parts of the Highlands of Scotland, the skyline observed from the top of high mountains reveals that the summit levels are all more or less at the same height; in fact the mountainous central Highlands are really part of a river-dissected

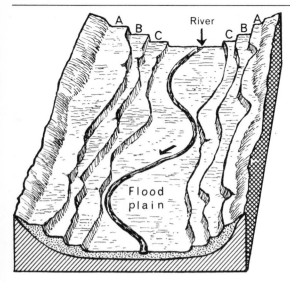

A, B, C – Terraces

Fig. 102. Periods of rejuvenation have left paired terraces AA, BB, and CC above the present flood-plain.

Fig. 103. Increased erosive activity due to uplift.

---

plateau which has recently been heavily glaciated. In other parts of highland Britain there are examples of the uplift of surfaces which had formerly been reduced to a peneplain. This is illustrated in Fig. 101, where rivers cut into the uplifted plateau and formed valleys, which were then enlarged by glacial action (p. 88). Now post-glacial rivers are again cutting into sediments in the valley bottom.

Rejuvenation Terraces

As a rejuvenated river cuts rapidly downwards, it can leave well-defined terraces along the valley sides. Such river terraces differ in location from meander terraces (p. 40), in that, due to the sudden accelerated erosion, they tend to be left 'paired'— at the same height on either side of the valley

(although complete terraces may not necessarily exist on both sides).

The completeness, or otherwise, of these relics of former flood-plains depends partly on processes of weathering and erosion, and partly on the continuing behaviour of the river itself. Some rivers in the south-west peninsula of England reveal by the positions of numerous terrace remnants and knick-points (p. 64), a long history of varying changes of land- and sea-levels.

A stand-still period may also allow meander terraces to be formed, and so further complicate the valley features.

Effects on the whole River Basin

We have seen that, as the river cuts downward at a greater rate, it gives extra energy to streams higher

in the basin, which in time have to fall further to reach their new local base-level.

This is illustrated in Fig. 103. The stream S1 in the main valley becomes entrenched; so that stream S2 must fall to the new level of S1, and so cuts further down into the landscape. In turn, the tributaries S3, and the gullies and rills G become more deeply incised. In these processes the gradient is first steepened where one stream meets another more active one, and this break of slope works its way back upstream by headward erosion (p. 36).

Changes in gradient which affect the main stream are thus very important to the nature of landforms in the whole basin; for this usually owes much to the erosive powers of a system of small streams.

The Formation of Canyons

Fig. 104. In the high eastern mountains and plateaux of South Africa rivers cut deep canyons, like this great trench cut through level-bedded rocks in the high country west of the Drakensberg. Notice the influence of the horizontal bedding on the landforms as high as H, and even on the distant slopes.

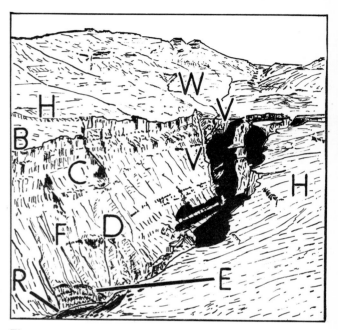

Fig. 105.

Under dry conditions, the sides of a canyon incised into resistant rock tend to remain steep. Only a few watercourses (W)—dry in the picture—cross the high level surface (H), and these continue as only minor valleys in the canyon side (V).

Here, level-bedded sandstones and lavas of differing resistance are exposed along the canyon walls (B, C, D), and the changing angles of slope show the resulting *differential erosion*. Some of the gentler slopes bear scree, and show close run-off channels (F). Far below, the river (R) is cutting downwards and still widening the valley—notice the undercutting below the slip at E.

Incised Meanders

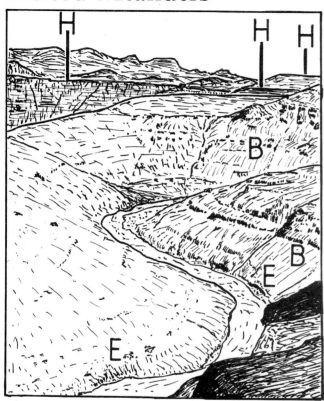

Fig. 106.

During the slow elevation of a plateau, a river may maintain its former course during the period of uplift, and even its meanders may become incised. Here, the shape of the winding valley itself, with the outcrops of horizontal beds (B), suggests that the river has long maintained its loops. Notice the evidence of present valley widening at E. In the background the different elevations of the high surfaces (H) suggest a number of marked changes, from time to time, in the rate of uplift of the landforms.

Fig. 107. An incised river in the high eastern mountains of South Africa, with wide loops in a valley of youthful narrowness.

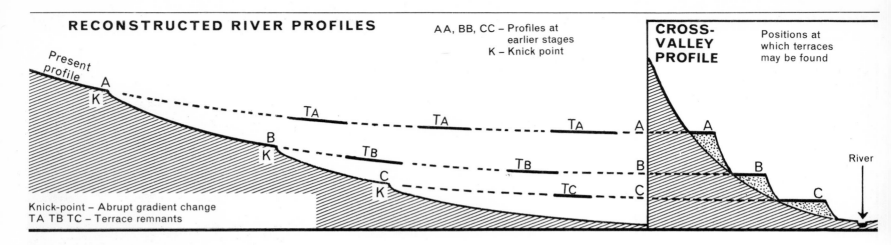

RECONSTRUCTED RIVER PROFILES

AA, BB, CC – Profiles at earlier stages
K – Knick point

CROSS-VALLEY PROFILE

Positions at which terraces may be found

Present profile

Knick-point – Abrupt gradient change
TA TB TC – Terrace remnants

River

Fig. 108. Sections downstream and across the lower valley show the positions of knick-points and possible terraces within the present valley.

Knick-points and Waterfalls

Where the gradient of a river is steepened because of the lowering of the base-level, a marked break of slope occurs at the *knick-point*, often with a short rapid or waterfall, which tends to work its way back upstream. The break of slope represents the point where the old profile of the river meets that of the newly graded one (Fig. 108). A series of knick-points along a river profile may indicate several successive lowerings of the base-level.

In Fig. 108 the oldest profile shown is that of the former valley floor AA. Hence it might be possible to find in the present valley remnants of a former floodplain and terraces at TA. A fall in base-level allowed the river to erode further and attain the profile BB, so that there may also be terrace remnants at TB; and, similarly at TC, related to the profile CC. It can be seen that the river is developing a new graded course below the third and lowest knick-point.

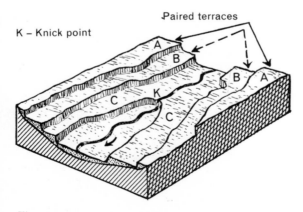

K – Knick point

Paired terraces

Fig. 109.

Fig. 109 shows more clearly how changes in level leave paired terraces, unlike the meander terraces on p. 40. In fact much depends on the rate of change of base-level, and the time which elapses between each period of change; for weathering or erosion may remove all or part of the earlier terraces, or greatly modify them. Fig. 109 should, therefore, be looked on as diagrammatic. Nevertheless knick-points may be recognised in the field and tell us much of the life history of the river system and the region it drains.

These are by no means the only cause of water-falls, as the following sections show. The way in which the face of the fall at the knick-point retreats is common to most waterfalls, and is illustrated in principle on p. 65. In Fig. 110 another particular type of fall, due to varying rock resistance, is shown.

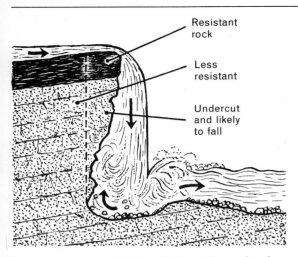

Fig. 110. A new vertical face will shortly be produced as the overhang collapses and the fall retreats.

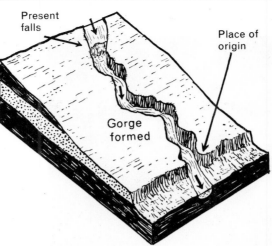

Fig. 111. Long-continued retreat leaves a steep-sided gorge.

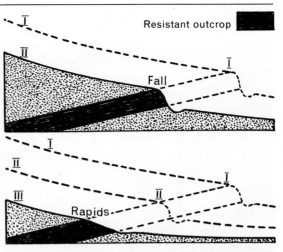

Fig. 112. Successive positions of falls, decreasing in height until only the rapids at the rocky outcrop disturb the almost graded profile.

Waterfalls

Where a river flows from a resistant to a less resistant rock, the latter may be worn down more quickly, and a more or less vertical face created. At the base of the falls a hollow may be excavated by abrasion, and as the water is very turbulent the rock face may be undercut. This is likely to happen fairly rapidly where the upper resistant rock is underlain by less resistant ones. As the cliff face collapses, the falls retreat upstream.

The successive retreat of a fall originating at a scarp face or plateau edge may lead to the formation of a long narrow gorge (Fig. 111). The rapid retreat of the Niagara Falls, averaging some 4 feet a year over thousands of years, has produced a gorge of this type seven miles long.

In some cases, as in Fig. 112, the falls may become less prominent as they retreat. From the former position I, where the river followed the profile I, the falls receded to position II. In time,

with the river almost 'at grade' (p. 40), position III is reached.

Eventually the only break in the profile will be the irregularities produced by this resistant outcrop, where the water cascades over rapids. Finally, with the elimination of falls and rapids, a graded profile is reached throughout. Not all falls decrease in height on retreat. Falls of the type shown in Fig. 111 may gain height as they recede, and the valley is extended into a high tableland.

In fact, waterfalls originate in many ways: tumbling from hanging valleys, or over cliffs, or plunging over fault scarps; and in young streams (Fig. 70) torrents fall steeply over the irregularities of their steep slopes. But whatever their origin, there is a tendency for the turbulent water to deepen the bed immediately downstream, and to cut back the higher surface immediately upstream.

Falls: The Influence of Structure

Fig. 113. Falls on the River Ure, in the upper part of Wensleydale, Yorkshire. Here at Aysgarth the river cascades over a long fall, or series of falls, in the form of steps.

Fig. 114.

The influence of rock structure on the nature of a fall is evident in the form of the stepped falls of the River Ure in the Yorkshire Pennines. This is seen in the photograph, and is shown from another viewpoint in Fig. 114.

In Fig. 113, low water exposes the steep face formed in the well-jointed rock, and the level bedding planes can still be seen above and below. In Fig. 114 the latter appear as the upper surfaces of a succession of level steps.

A Fall Recedes

Fig. 115.

Here, again, during a dry period, relatively little water tumbles over the fall, exposing, in this case, much of the face of the fall (F). It also shows the rock debris (D) at the base, which has fallen from the retreating face. Behind this, spray rises from the deeper plunge-pool (P) at the foot of the fall.

Notice within the narrow valley the sheer, much jointed rocks (J). The walls retain their steepness as blocks fall from the undercut face and the sides.

Fig. 116. Thomson's Falls in the Highlands of Kenya plunging from the upper, level surface have developed a very long steep-sided gorge, typical of a receding fall of this kind.

Part III   Arid and Semi-Arid Landforms

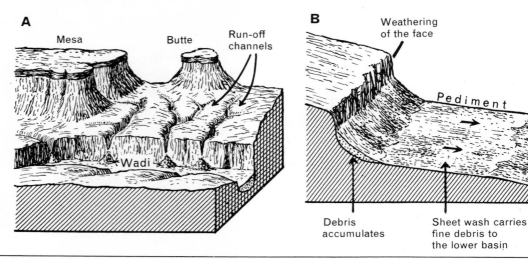

Fig. 117. In A the storm water is concentrated in channels. In B a thin sheet of water floods over the gently sloping pediment, removing weathered material from the base of the retreating plateau edge.

In arid and semi-arid conditions, where the water deficiency tends to lead to an incomplete vegetation cover, the landforms often present a striking difference to those of a humid landscape.

Water Action

It is evident that many features are, perhaps surprisingly, the result of the action of running water—either caused by torrents, which follow the occasional violent storm acting on bare surfaces, or perhaps created initially by the surface water of an earlier, wetter period and modified by the desert storms of today.

The heavy downpours are drained away in different ways, mainly by two contrasting types of run-off. On gently sloping surfaces—such as occur on many of the tropical dry plateau lands, in Africa, Australia, the Americas, and parts of south-east Asia—a sheet of flood water surges

over the surface, eroding little, but carrying away a great volume of loose debris towards river valleys or into inland basins or salt lakes. On steeper slopes, rills take the rapid run-off into gullies, and thence into steep-sided valleys (wadis, or canyons), there being little to hamper the flow in the way of soils and vegetation. Here the water may rise so rapidly that it tears down these main channels as *flash floods*. The run-off from each storm follows the same courses, and the valleys become ever deeper and wider—though the dry conditions help to maintain the steep sides (p. 60), and much alluvium is left on the bed as the flow ceases.

As the wadis open onto lower country, the flood water tends to spread out and drop the load of gravel and sand. Sometimes the streams fall into inland depressions and build up great alluvial fans of heavy material at the edge of such basins. The fans may coalesce to form a more or less continuous slope of debris, known as a *bahada*. Some basins

may become slowly filled with such material.

The water itself often flows into inland saline lakes, or sinks into sands or salt flats, and is eventually lost by evaporation. In Fig. 116, the river which cascades over the Thomson's Falls in Kenya is seen during low water. In flood a great torrent thunders continuously over these falls—but none of this reaches the sea. It is lost by evaporation and seepage as it flows northwards into the arid inland parts of northern Kenya.

The sheet wash shown in Fig. 117 B fundamentally affects the nature of landforms on semi-arid tablelands. Periodic heavy rains remove debris from beneath escarpments, allowing the whole face to be exposed to weathering. Sheet wash carries fine debris away, causing little erosion, so that escarpments and relic hills stand sheer above gently sloping plains. These are characteristic features of many semi-arid landscapes. The evolution of the landforms depends on the balance between the rates of weathering and removal of debris.

Water Courses in a Desert Landscape

Fig. 118 clearly illustrates the extent to which running water may alter the whole face of the landscape in a normally arid climate, where bare rock is unprotected through the lack of vegetation and top soil; though the drainage patterns may have been established under wetter conditions.

In the main wadi can be seen the remains of the load carried in times of flood and left, as the waters subsided, as a thick filling covering the bed. In places the channels and terraces of successive floods are visible, and lines of small deep-rooted bushes tap the water-table, far below.

The main wadis are cut deep into the gently sloping plateau surfaces; across these, smaller, winding channels carry storm waters, which have also made deep incisions in places along the steep edges of the wadis.

Stream courses cut across the edges of the parallel bedding planes exposed on the retreating plateau faces. To the left of the main wadi can be seen projecting ridges, remnants of a higher surface removed by the headward erosion of a series of channels draining to the various wadis.

Fig. 118. The Sahra el-Arabiya, in eastern Egypt, seen from 10,000 feet, reveals the patterns of dry water channels (wadis); these carry the water which runs over the surface during the very occasional heavy storms.

Residual Hills

Fig. 119. Part of the Olduvai Gorge in northern Tanzania, cut through the clays, sands, and volcanic ash, down to lava flows of nearly two million years ago. It is here, in the lower levels, that Professor Leakey and his wife have uncovered the remains of 'Zinjanthropus Man', dated as some 1,750,000 years old.

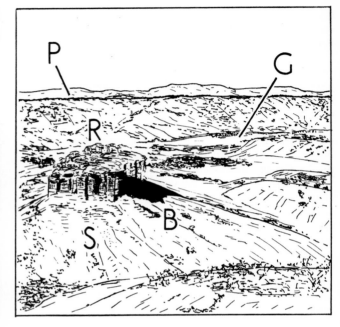

Fig. 120.

This outstanding feature of red, level-bedded rocks, is part of a larger mass left by the creation of a system of river valleys draining to the main gorge (G). The gorge is formed in the plateau whose surface (P) is indicated. Weathering has caused the sides of the residual hill (R) to retreat with almost vertical upper slopes. Beneath, remains of the once more extensive lower beds (B) outcrop on the gentler lower slopes, mantled with screes (S) of varying coarseness. There are signs of fairly recent water erosion on the slopes; but debris protects the lower strata from more drastic effects of weathering. The form of the whole feature is characteristic of residual hills found in semi-arid and arid landscapes, with the steep upper slopes and more gentle lower ones, where the debris is not readily removed.

Residual Hills

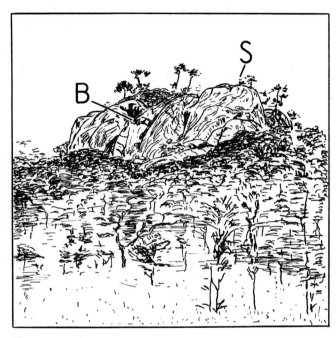

Fig. 121.

Fig. 122. An outstanding mass of disintegrating rock rises from the closely wooded savannah in southern Kenya. From its summit scores of other residual hills of this type may be seen.

Many inselbergs of resistant crystalline rock stand out steep-sided above the plateaux of central Africa. They are the smaller remnants of blocks which have been detached by erosion from the retreating edges of higher surfaces, and have become progressively reduced in size.

The smoothness of the upper surfaces (S) resemble the exfoliated rock seen in Fig. 4. The angular blocks which are seen at B, and which lie about the base of the hill, result from splitting along the joints or foliation planes, and fall under the pull of gravity. The name 'kopje', or sometimes 'castle kopje', is also applied to this type of residual hill in southern Africa.

Wind Erosion and Deposition

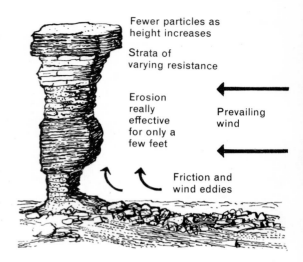

Fewer particles as height increases

Strata of varying resistance

Erosion really effective for only a few feet

Prevailing wind

Friction and wind eddies

Fig. 123. A pillar undercut by wind erosion. Friction with the ground reduces wind speed and erosion at very low levels, but eddies develop. Most erosion takes place a little above, where there are the greatest number of particles (and, in the diagram, less resistant rock). At higher levels there are fewer particles, unless in exceptional sandstorms.

Residual Hills

The landforms of the arid regions tend to show much greater contrasts of slope than those formed under humid conditions. Gently sloping pediments give way suddenly to abrupt plateau edges or steep isolated hills. Deep narrow wadis may cut through level plateaux, above which rise steep-sided mesas or buttes (Fig. 117). The latter, relics of higher surfaces, are often capped with a layer of resistant rock, so that the upper slopes are particularly steep, while screes give more gentle slopes at the base.

In some cases, especially on the plateaux of the African savannah lands, isolated rocky masses of hard coarse-grained rocks are all that remain of the former higher surface. It is thought that as plateau edges retreat by weathering, and the removal of the weathered debris by sheet-wash, ultimately there must be just a residual knob— an *inselberg*. Even that, subject to exfoliation (p. 12) and other weathering, is likely to vanish eventually. Figs. 4 and 122 show examples of outstanding residual hills of this type.

Wind Action

Erosion

Weathering, and especially long-continued expansion and contraction, reduces boulders and pebbles to even smaller sizes. Small sand particles, which result, can be carried by the wind. Their removal is known as *deflation*, and is, of course, an important process in the absence of vegetation.

Deflation may lower a whole surface in time. Depressions, or deflation basins, may be excavated by wind action. Many are shallow, but some, like Egypt's Qattara Depression, are hundreds of feet deep, and only limited in depth by the water-table.

Many desert surfaces are of windswept rock, perhaps covered by boulders and pebbles too big to be transported—a surface known as *reg*.

At low levels, wind-borne particles act as tools of erosion. By attrition (p. 33) they polish each other, creating smooth faces and sharp edges. The lower parts of cliff faces and pillars may be fretted by wind abrasion, as lines of weakness are picked out (Fig. 123).

Deposition

Wind eddies may pick up sand grains and cause them to advance in forward hops near the surface; or strong winds may transport fine particles en masse, as in dust storms. Sand so moved may be deposited as ripples or ridges, or accumulate to form *dunes*, of which the most common form is the *barchan (barkhan)*, with the 'horns' of its crescent shape carried forward down-wind. Their size varies greatly. Fig. 127 shows a low isolated dune some thirty feet in height: those in Fig. 125 are twice as high, and in southern Arabia many rise to over a hundred feet.

72

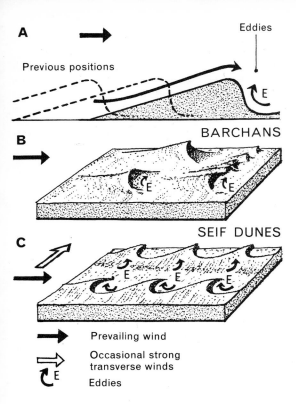

A
Previous positions
Eddies
E

BARCHANS
B
E E

SEIF DUNES
C
E E E
E E E

Prevailing wind

Occasional strong
transverse winds

E Eddies

Fig. 124. A shows a barchan advancing, and B and C the relation of barchans and seif dunes to the winds.

Sand may also accumulate against low obstructions, or where the wind lull in the lee of larger obstacles causes deposition. Once formed, the dune may grow larger. But sand carried forward up the long windward upslope slips or falls in the lee, where eddies tend to maintain a steep face; so that the whole mass moves slowly forward.

Apart from the crescent-shaped barchans, there may be long *seif dunes*, built up where winds from two directions dominate and tend to elongate the ridges. Eddies keep the surface between the lines of dunes fairly clear and build up their sides.

Deposition and Accumulation

Fig. 125. A composite dune in Death Valley, California. Notice the smooth windward slope of the upper surface and the steep lee-face.

Even here there are signs of the occasional presence of water, in the occurrence of vegetation and in the cracked, mud-caked surface in the small hollow in the foreground.

73

Desert Landscapes

The outcrop in the foreground, split and peeling, with rounded upper surfaces, shows many of the characteristics of rocks exposed to desert conditions. The expansion and contraction, caused by the high surface temperatures by day and the rapid fall in temperature at night, possibly combined with condensation and chemical effects—for the desert air is by no means completely dry—lead to the fracturing which has obviously occurred. The sheer, newly exposed faces are lighter in appearance; for long exposure may build up brown or black films on the rock, as small quantities of dissolved matter are brought to the surface—some, with iron oxide, remain as 'desert varnish', while other salts are blown away.

The rocks are apt to stand bare in sand deserts such as this, for the particles in the dust-laden winds tend to be carried around outstanding obstacles by the air flow; for this reason the work of wind as an eroding agent is often less effective than one would think.

Sand accumulates on the lower slopes and gradually extends up the side of the rocks. Notice the presence of vegetation even in such dry conditions, and how coarse grasses manage to survive along the valley bottom: their root systems are often widespread, and where sand does not drift too much, they act as dune 'fixers'.

Fig. 126. The Western Desert in Upper Egypt. Desert scenery in which the disintegration of the rocks and the deposition of the products of disintegration—sand—appear as typical processes.

A Barchan

Fig. 127. An unusual site for a barchan, in that it is derived from sand particles carried from the dry surface of the savannah of northern Tanzania, not far from the great Olduvai Gorge (Fig. 119). Here the plateau surface is dry and loose, grazed over by Masai cattle and pounded by hundreds of thousands of zebra and wildebeest, so that, as can be seen, there is much bare soil exposed to the drying winds. The barchan shows the typical 'horns' and steep slope of the lee face, and the long, smooth upslope on the windward side, from which it has moved a considerable distance.

Gulleys Formed in an Arid Landscape

This dramatically eroded scenery borders the large valley which lies below sea-level, and whose floor is extensively covered by salt accumulations. Like other inland basins, there are, along the edges, coarse fans of alluvial materials deposited by streams which have acquired a heavy load during flood periods and left much of it where the abrupt change of slope occurs: such fans may grow to form continuous expanding ridges of loose, dry materials.

Here the effects of storm run-off on dry, easily eroded sediments are obvious. Notice the rills on each ridge, the deep gulleying, and the places where the occasional main water channel cuts through, like the winding course at bottom, left. Other main channels are indicated by the direction and slopes of the serried rows of gullied ridges.

Normally, the presence of vegetation acts to bind the soil, and offers physical protection. Here there is no soil in the strict sense and, of course, no vegetation, so that the impact of the very occasional heavy downpours is not lessened in any way.

Fig. 128. A desolate landscape in Death Valley, California. A deep trench, some 280 feet below sea-level, it is one of the most arid parts of America, with very high summer temperatures and extremely low humidity; isolated storms may therefore have drastic effects.

Weathering Under Desert Conditions

On the Mongolian plains the lack of cloud cover for much of the year allows a rapid gain of radiant heat during the long summer days, when the sun's altitude is high, and high surface temperatures result. During the winter months, and at night, the rapid loss of radiant heat produces low temperatures; and the large diurnal temperature range, especially in summer, means that the surface rocks are often under stress and strain. The breakdown by weathering can rapidly reduce outstanding rocks, like this remnant of a former surface.

The flat, hard-capped top stands several hundred feet above the present plains, and other relics of this former surface can be seen beyond. Notice the opened joints, the peeling of the rocks, the collections of loose scree, and the wind ripples on the accumulation of smaller sand particles, which tend to be sorted by wind from coarser debris.

Fig. 129. The flat-topped relic of a former surface stands above the arid, stony plains of Outer Mongolia, subjected to severe weathering in a region which experiences extremes of temperature. Below, the remnants of this reduced butte break down beside it on the rocky pediment.

Part IV   Glaciation

The following pages illustrate the ways in which moving masses of ice, such as are found in the great polar ice-sheets and as valley glaciers amid high mountains, can drastically alter the landforms; and also show how they may affect landscapes far from the actual region of glaciation.

The Nature of the Glacier Ice

The sun's heat causes some surface melting, and winds ◀aid evaporation from the surface.

The glacier itself is formed by the processes described on p. 81. Fig. 130 shows that the upper layers of the ice contain air, and have a granular texture (névé ice). Bands in the ◀upper ice show seasonal gains—rather like tree rings.

Under pressure the lower layers become glassy, and ◀able to 'flow'.

Beneath the glacier the pressure is very great, and the temperature of the lower ice is near its melting point. In fact, melt-water usually runs freely down-valley beneath the mass of ice.

Fig. 130. A crevasse in a Swiss valley glacier shows the changes in the nature of the ice with depth.

Snowfields and Ice Movement

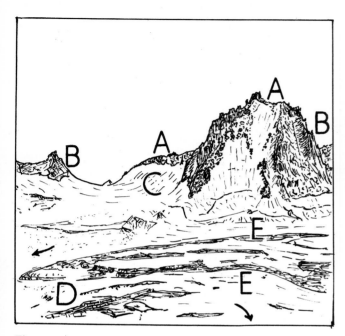

Fig. 131.

Where the Glacier Starts

Notice the frost-shattered peaks (A). By day the sun melts some of the surface snow, and also some of the ice in cracks in the rocks. By night the water there freezes and expands, forcing the rock apart and shattering peaks by detaching loosened blocks. These jagged peaks clearly show the powerful action of this form of weathering, which emphasises the joints and cracks in the rocks.

The shadows suggest that the bare mountain sides at B receive more sun than the side C, where snow remains high on the slope. Notice the layering at D, where compacted snow moves away and slips forward, as the ice beneath flows in the directions shown by the arrows.

Fig. 132. More snow accumulates each year than can melt, so that glacier ice is formed beneath. As this moves away it speeds up, causing cracks and crevasses to appear (E). In this zone of accumulation, high in the Alps, these show up as surface snow slips.

Valley Glaciers

CORRIE BASIN

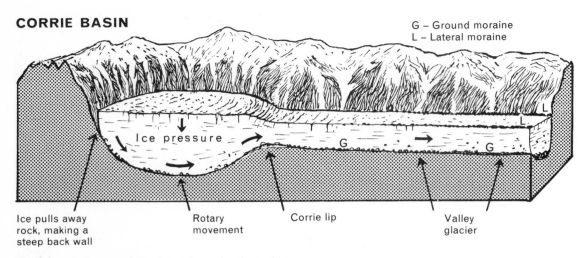

G – Ground moraine
L – Lateral moraine

Ice pressure

Ice pulls away rock, making a steep back wall

Rotary movement

Corrie lip

Valley glacier

Fig. 133. A tongue of ice flows from the deepening hollow. On the surface are lines of *lateral* (side) *moraine* (L), rock debris fallen onto the ice from the weathered valley sides. Beneath the ice is *ground moraine* (G).

CORRIE AND CORRIE LAKE

Steep back wall

Arête

LAKE

Overflow channel

Lip

Fig. 134. Beyond the corrie a narrow ridge, known as an *arête*, separates it from another glacial valley.

Where the Glacier Starts

Fig. 130 shows how the annual snow accumulation can turn into glacial ice, and that great thicknesses may be built up. Snow and the ice formed from it cannot accumulate indefinitely in a mountain basin. Eventually, increasing pressure of ice causes part of the mass to move downslope and to flow slowly to lower levels. In time, and with continued accumulations of snow, the ice may advance a considerable way down an existing valley.

As more ice moves from the place of origin, the whole ice-mass in the basin tends to rotate, and eventually wears a deep hollow, with the help of abrasion by rocks frozen into the base of the ice.

Some of the ice freezes on to the back wall of the basin and, as it moves forward, plucks rock away,

causing the wall to be worn back and eventually leaving a steep face. The final result is an 'armchair' feature known as a *corrie* or *cirque*.

Under the pressure created by further accumulation at the source, the tongue of ice which has moved over the 'lip' of the corrie now flows down the valley, plucking rock from the valley sides and floor; and with the aid of rock debris (known as *moraine*) at the base, the great weight of ice grinds against, and deepens, the valley floor.

Long after the glaciers have vanished, the results of their action are left as easily recognisable features of the landscape. High mountains, the source of many ice-flows, contain numerous 'arm-chair' corries, like that above.

Today the base of such hollows often contains water, forming a deep corrie lake, or *tarn*. The overflow stream may cut a channel through the lip of the corrie and then plunge down the valley as a waterfall, or in a series of falls. The complete armchair shape may be masked by weathered material from the walls, which builds up scree slopes inside.

Multiple Corries

Sometimes a number of glaciers flow from basins on several sides of a mountain mass, and a pair of steep-walled corries may be separated only by the narrow knife-edge ridge known as an *arête*.

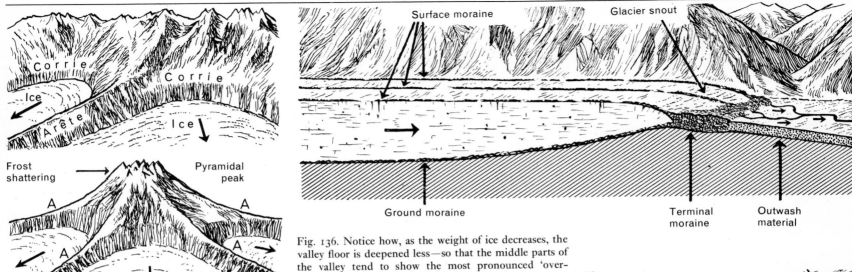

Fig. 135. Headward erosion by the ice.

Fig. 136. Notice how, as the weight of ice decreases, the valley floor is deepened less—so that the middle parts of the valley tend to show the most pronounced 'over-deepening'.

Occasionally a mountain mass is considerably reduced as corrie formation, and erosion of the back wall, proceed on several sides. Between the back-to-back corries the mountain is left as a *pyramidal peak*, with branching arêtes (A), and the upper heights showing the effects of frost-shattering.

The Ice Moves Down-Valley

As it moves, the ice moulds itself to the valley profile. It plucks away rock, scratches and smooths the sides, and deepens the valley itself. Spurs jutting across its path are in time eroded away, and stretches of the valley straightened.

The forward movement of ice is continuous, as a greater weight is added at the source; but eventually a position is reached in the valley where the rate of melting is so great that all the ice arriving melts. At this location the tapering front of the ice, or the 'snout' of the glacier, is continuously receiving morainic material, which can be carried no further and so builds up as a *terminal moraine* across the valley (Fig. 136). Some of this debris is redistributed down-valley as 'outwash' by the melt water and by streams from the ice face. There may, of course, be periodic, annual, and seasonal variation in the amount of ice accumulating at the source, and in the rate of melting: so that the position of the snout of the glacier may vary accordingly.

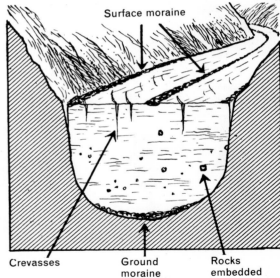

Fig. 137. The typical U-shaped profile, showing surface- and ground-moraine and rocks embedded in the ice.

81

Cirque (Corrie) Basins

Fig. 138. A team of surveyors move up against the flow of the main glacier (G). Beyond, ice flows from beneath the snowfield, seen in a broad corrie basin (C).

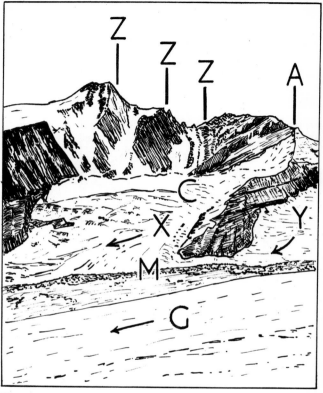

Fig. 139.

Ice, covered by recent snow, is flowing in two streams X and Y from high catchment areas towards the main glacier (G). A narrow arête (A) separates the two sources of glacial ice.

Beyond the climbers can be seen a zone of debris, or moraine (M), with a line of heavy material fallen onto the main ice from the valley sides further up.

An examination of the mountain sides shows how weathering and erosion have acted on the jointed rocks and emphasised the planes of bedding and the tilt of the strata (Z).

The Corrie in Post-Glacial Times

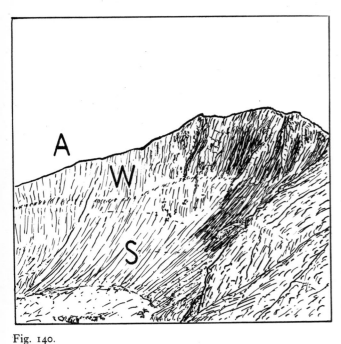

Fig. 140.

Fig. 141. This great cirque (corrie) in Snowdonia, north Wales, was formed by the rotation of ice moving forward from the bowl-shaped catchment area. The plucking of rock from the enclosing walls has left the sheer, bare faces too steep to allow a soil-covering or vegetation.

Compare this with Fig. 138 opposite. It is easy to see the similarities and to picture the scene when this huge cirque was filled with ice, and covered with surface snow. At this time the headward erosion, mainly by plucking, produced the steep back wall (W).

The processes of weathering help to maintain the steepness of the upper slopes. But as the stones rattle down and collect as scree (S), at a natural angle of repose, the lower slopes are more gentle.

The knife-edge wall on the far side separates two glacially formed valleys, and is thus an arête (A).

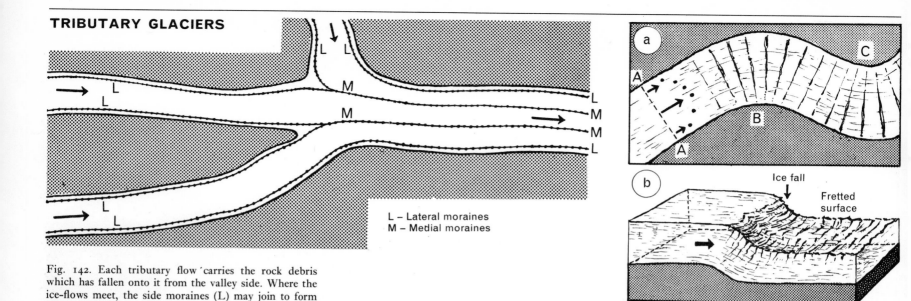

L – Lateral moraines
M – Medial moraines

Fig. 142. Each tributary flow carries the rock debris which has fallen onto it from the valley side. Where the ice-flows meet, the side moraines (L) may join to form middle (medial) moraines (M). These, with the other rock material beneath, or embedded in the ice are carried forward to where the glacier melts.

Fig. 143. Poles indicate the relative rates of movement of near-surface ice; cracks, crevasses, and fretted surfaces are natural indicators.

While Ice Fills the Valley

The amount of ice moving down-valley may be increased by tributaries, as in a flowing river system. The pressure of the ice on the valley bed and the rate of flow of the main glacier may thus be increased, so that the valley floor is often deepened still more downstream of tributaries. The presence of existing knicks or falls in the valley bed, or the action of ice in plucking away bands of weaker rock from the bed, may also cause the valley floor to become deepened. A narrowing of the valley also acts to increase the speed of ice flow, which again makes for further deepening of the valley floor.

The near-surface flow of ice tends to be fastest in mid-stream, and a series of posts driven into the ice and aligned across the valley (AA) will in time indicate the relatively faster movement in the centre, as shown in Fig. 143.

Bends in the valley also affect the rate of movement. Fig. 143 (a) shows that there is a tendency for cracks or crevasses to open out where the ice moves faster in one place than another, at the outside of the valley bend (B). As the same effect occurs on the reverse curve (C), the cracks now tend to close up again, though the surface usually remains fretted.

Fig. 143 (b) shows that where a step occurs in a valley floor, cracks and crevasses develop; and a rough surface results from the speeding up of ice as it forms an ice-fall, followed by slower movement lower down. Figs. 144, 145 and 148 show such a broken surface, typical of the longer glaciers. It is instructive to study the scenery of mountain country in which glaciers are still active. Since the last Ice Age was at its maximum the glaciers have usually shrunk, so that a combination of glacial and post-glacial features are visible. For this reason, Fig. 144 repays careful study.

Valley Glacier: The Moving Ice

Make a simple outline sketch of the physical features shown in Fig. 144, and as an aid to observation:

1. Mark on the multiple corries where snow accumulates and glacier ice forms.

2. Identify a number of residual, frost-shattered peaks.

3. Indicate truncated spurs along the valley sides (use Fig. 151 as a guide).

4. Show where weathered material is accumulating at the base of the mountains.

5. Mark on the area where outwash from the glacial moraine has been deposited, and some of the channels which are incised in this alluvial material.

6. Comment on the shape of the hill at bottom left.

7. Indicate post-glacial features of the landscape.

8. Consider evidence that this fast-moving glacier has occupied a much greater volume than it does now. Suggest why, as in so many glaciated areas in similar latitudes, the size of the glaciers and effects of glaciation have been particularly great on the west side of the land masses.

Fig. 144. The Franz Joseph glacier flows from a number of ice sources among the high Southern Alps of New Zealand. The glacier descends through thick bush to under 700 feet above sea-level.

Valley Glacier

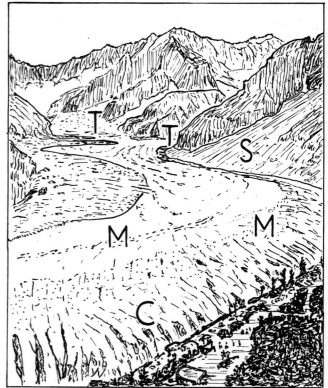

Fig. 146.

Fig. 145 shows the boulder-strewn surface of a glacier occupying a winding mountain valley. Notice the following features:

S: the scree slope formed from material weathered from the valley sides.

M: surface moraine made up of this fallen material—the middle lines of moraine coming from tributary ice, higher up.

C: deep crevasses, opened up on the outside of the bend.

T: the former valley spurs which were worn back—truncated—when the ice level was higher.

Fig. 145. The Mer de Glace, one of the great Alpine glaciers.

Tributary Glaciers

Fig. 147.

Fig. 148. In high Alpine country, snow collects wherever the slopes are gentle enough to retain it, as high up on the right of this mountain mass. Here, in the foreground, ice is converging from several small corries and flowing down a fall to join the main glacier below.

Looking down the ice-fall (I), we see:

F: the fretted surface, where crevasses have opened up as the ice moves over the fall.

M: the lines of moraine from the main and tributary glaciers.

S: the collection of scree on the hillsides.

C: the high corries where small tongues of ice or glaciers are formed.

Here, as in the other pictures, the jaggedness of the peaks, heavily weathered under these climatic conditions, are typical of glaciated mountain country.

Valley Glaciation

PRE-GLACIAL VALLEY

Fig. 149. Before and after glaciation.

POST-GLACIAL VALLEY

(Scree slopes and fans omitted).

Fig. 150. The valley floor after glaciation.

After the Ice has Gone

Many parts of Highland Britain, such as the Lake District and the Scottish Highlands, have been modified by long periods of mountain glaciation. Nowhere in Europe are there now extensive Ice Caps, but high mountains like the Alps and Pyrenees still contain permanent snowfields and glaciers.

It is important to realise that while in some regions both mountains and lowlands were covered, and much altered, by extensive ice-sheets, in other mountainous regions ice-altered landforms are to be seen chiefly in the valleys. But though glacier ice may only have moved down the valleys, the adjacent highlands usually show the effects of severe weathering at that time and since—especially the results of frost-shattering, which is highly destructive of exposed rock surfaces at high altitudes. The following pages show many mountain

features resulting from glaciation which are now typical parts of the scenery; yet most of these are transitory on a geological time-scale—for everyday processes of weathering and erosion in humid climates tend to modify them extremely rapidly.

Fig. 149 shows the transformation of a young pre-glacial river valley by erosion, both during and after occupation by a glacier.

The valley spurs have been truncated, and a broad U-shaped valley now runs through the mountains. In fact, the post-glacial river is seen winding its way across a flat-floored valley; for a new alluvial flood-plain obliterates the lower U-shape, and covers, perhaps, glacially formed steps in the valley bed, and hides various glacial deposits.

Not all valley floors are masked by recent alluvium; and many still display the moraines and outwash left as the snout of the glacier retreated under warmer conditions.

Where the glacier snout remained fairly station-

ary for some time, the moraine carried forward by the ice was built into a sizeable cross-valley barrier (M) (Figs. 150 and 153). The material washed out by melt waters may linger in some places in the valley as deltaic mounds (D), especially where a stream outlet remained in one position for a long period.

Fig. 150 also indicates diagrammatically a step (S) in the valley floor. Such an abrupt change in level may have been created when ice erosion at the base of the glacier emphasised differences in rock structure by wearing and plucking away the weaker rock downstream—somewhat in the manner of the waterfall (p. 65). Or it may have been initiated by an addition in weight of glacier ice by the contribution of a tributary glacier: this would have increased the deepening process downstream and so left a marked step in the base of the valley. In a hard, resistant rock such a step may remain in post-glacial times.

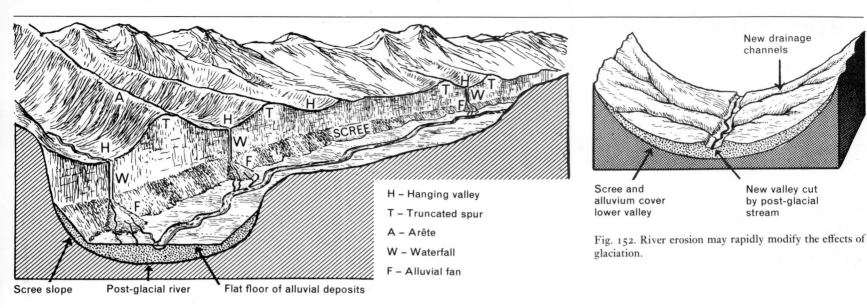

H – Hanging valley

T – Truncated spur

A – Arête

W – Waterfall

F – Alluvial fan

Scree slope   Post-glacial river   Flat floor of alluvial deposits

Fig. 151. The actions of glaciation, weathering, and flowing water combine to produce the typical features of the post-glacial valley.

Scree and alluvium cover lower valley   New valley cut by post-glacial stream

New drainage channels

Fig. 152. River erosion may rapidly modify the effects of glaciation.

Hanging Valleys

The tributary glaciers which flowed into the main glacier lacked the weight to deepen their valleys to the same extent as the latter. They certainly produced the same straightening and rounded cross-valley profile as the main flow, however; and now that the ice has retreated, the mouths of these tributary valleys open out high up above the floor of the main valley (H in Fig. 151)—*hanging valleys* with a steep drop beneath.

Streams from hanging valleys, therefore, cascade as waterfalls into the main valley, and tend to build up alluvial fans of coarse material along the valley sides.

The Main Valley

Fig. 151 shows how the spurs of the former river valley were worn back by the ice (T—*truncated spur*). In post-glacial times the sides have been subjected to weathering, and there is often a well-marked slope of scree extending up the valley side. The screes have the angle of repose of the fallen rock, and produce a break of slope which is usually a characteristic feature of the valley profile—in fact the more gentle side-slope of a glaciated 'U' valley is often that of scree.

The Post-Glacial Drainage

Present snow-melt, mountain streams and waterfalls feed the new post-glacial river. Frequently, as illustrated in Figs. 149 and 151, the river winds its way across a flat alluvial plain in the widened valley, behaving as any river in the plain stage, and perhaps forming a delta in a valley lake which acts as its base-level (Figs. 160 and 163).

Sometimes, however, where the base-level is much lower, the post-glacial river cuts a new narrow valley in the floor of the larger glaciated one, and leaves remnants of the old floor as higher terraces. This is seen in Fig. 152, where the new valley is formed in post-glacial deposits.

After the Ice has Gone

Fig. 153. A massive terminal moraine forms a barrier across a formerly glaciated valley in the Alps. Here, the only remains of the extensive ice covering at the height of the last glacial period are the now small tongues of ice (T) on the slopes of the high mountains.

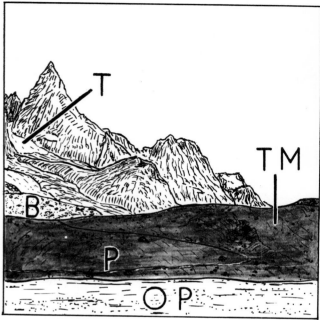

Fig. 154.

This whole, large, cross-valley barrier is built of morainic deposits which accumulated year after year at the snout of a glacier. Its height is emphasised by that of the trees and by the winding path, P.

Notice the large boulders carried along and deposited by the ice—best seen on the boulder strewn slope, B.

In front of the terminal moraine (TM) is the finer material of the outwash plain (OP), now bearing grass and a carpet of flowers.

The steepness of the slopes of the mountain masses beyond is partly due to the angle at which the rocks themselves are tilted.

A Typically 'U' Shaped Valley

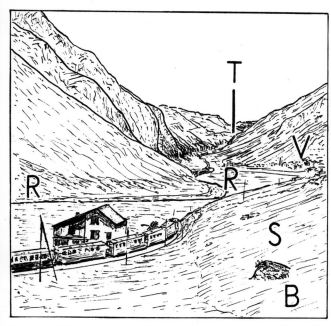

Fig. 155. Diagrammatic—without the tree cover: to indicate the effects of glaciation, weathering, and the action of the post-glacial river. In the background, some of the valley infilling has been removed in the diagram, to emphasise the truncation of the slopes, which is clearly seen as you travel along the valley.

Notice the clearly defined 'U' shaped profile, and the truncated spurs (T).

The village, V, here lies on a terrace and on the gentler slopes above the floor of the valley, through which the river RR, seen in the left foreground, now flows.

In fact, part of the curve of the lower 'U' slopes are due to modification by screes. Notice in the foreground the scree slope S, shown by the different tone of green, and the fallen boulders projecting, like that in the foreground (B).

Fig. 156. Valley glaciers have, by their erosive action, provided mountain regions with fine through-routes of communication. There is now no interference from obstructive spurs, though the roads and railways have to keep to the valley sides to avoid much bridging of post-glacial rivers, and to make use of firmer terrain. Villages, too, use the elevation of screes and fans.

Overdeepened Valleys and Glacial Lakes

D – Delta
H – Hanging valley
T – Terminal moraine

Fig. 157. The outlet of a glacial ribbon lake.

Outlet from the lake
flows over the old
outwash plain

As we have seen, the moving ice deepened especially the middle parts of the valley, between source and snout. Downstream of hanging valleys, where tributary ice gave added momentum, or where bands of weaker rock in the bed have been plucked away, there may be particularly deep portions. In some valleys these have later been filled by streams bearing run-off, or melt water, to form the present long, narrow lakes, which, taking the shape of the valley, are often known as *ribbon lakes*.

Where the overdeepened troughs reach the coast below the present sea-level, deep inlets, with shallow entrances, known as *fiords*, extend inland (pp. 149 and 150).

Fig. 157 shows the lower end of a glacial ribbon lake occupying a valley which has been overdeepened. The valley is shown as typically shallowing towards the position where the glacial snout had remained for long periods (revealed by the lines of terminal moraine). A step in the valley floor shows the extra deepening due to the additional weight of tributary ice which once occupied the present hanging valley (H).

The moraines (T) act as a barrier, though the overflow from the lake escapes down-valley by the outlet cut through the morainic ridges.

A waterfall from the hanging valley (H) has provided material for an alluvial fan below, and this is now extending into the lake in the form of a small delta (D).

The English Lake District and Scottish Highlands are among the many glaciated mountain regions with numerous deep ribbon lakes—Windermere some 200 feet deep, and Loch Morar over 1,000 feet deep at the maximum. The pre-glacial drainage system in the Lake District developed radially, following uplift which raised the whole structure to form a dome. The present lakes, therefore, lie in the radial pattern of the rivers, and, of course, occupy portions of their heavily glaciated valleys. Such lakes are relatively transient features of the landscape.

The Temporary Nature of the Lakes

A long, narrow ribbon lake which is bounded by high valley sides and fed by streams from mountainous regions, is likely to receive a great amount of alluvium as well, and also scree and washed out material from the slopes.

The result is that the in-filling is very rapid, when considered in terms of geological time, and the existence of the lake is threatened from the moment of formation, as we have already seen in the case of other lakes (p. 53).

Fig. 158 shows how a river, or rivers, at the head of the valley almost always build up an alluvial plain, which is often an area of valuable agricultural occupation in such mountainous country.

Further down the valley, the alluvial material brought down by strong post-glacial streams is deposited by the sudden check in flow as it enters the lake. This gradually builds up until, in the case of streams on opposite sides of the valley, their

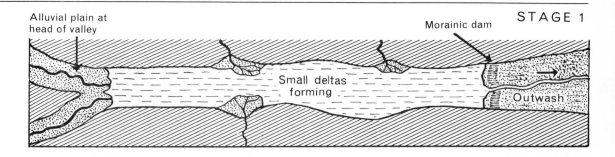

Alluvial plain at head of valley

Morainic dam

STAGE 1

Small deltas forming

Outwash

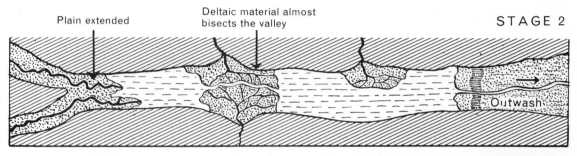

Plain extended

Deltaic material almost bisects the valley

STAGE 2

Outwash

Fig. 158. The division of a lake by deltaic infilling.

deltas extend right across the lake.

In this way the ribbon lake may virtually be divided into two smaller ones, as has happened in the case of Bassenthwaite and Derwentwater in the English Lake District. The very nature of ribbon lakes makes them particularly prone to this, and to infilling by debris which falls from the steep slopes above—as in the case of the great screes in Fig. 163, with extensive accumulations both above and below lake level.

Another way in which the lakes may disappear, as such, is by drainage through a river channel which has been cut downward to such an extent as to tap the waters of the lake at ever lower levels; see also p. 53. This may well occur where the lake is far above sea-level and the lower river is fed by strong tributaries, which cause it to degrade very rapidly and speed its headward erosion. Fig. 159 shows that a river may continue to entrench itself in the landscape and may ultimately drain the lake completely.

Infilling

Lake outlet
S   R

River

LAKE PROFILE

Later profile of riverbed

Fig. 159. The outlet river is able to drain the lake waters at R, and later, by cutting downward and headward, at S.

Glacial Lakes

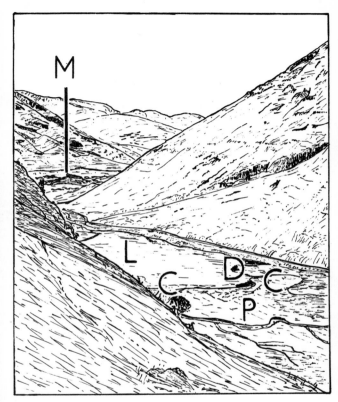

Fig. 161.

Here the former glaciers have affected the whole landscape. Their action can be seen in the plucked and rounded hill features—part of an old river-dissected plateau—and in the broad glaciated valleys.

The lake (L) occupies an over-deepened hollow, which is being filled in by alluvium carried by the water channels (C). Much of the deltaic material (D) at the head of the lake quickly acquires vegetation, which helps to consolidate the new, flat plain (P) advancing down the valley.

Morainic mounds (M) lie in the broad valley beyond.

Fig. 160. A glacier carved this broad 'U' shaped valley along a former river course in the Scottish Highlands, amid a landscape of hard, resistant rock, plucked and smoothed by ice-action.

A Ribbon Lake

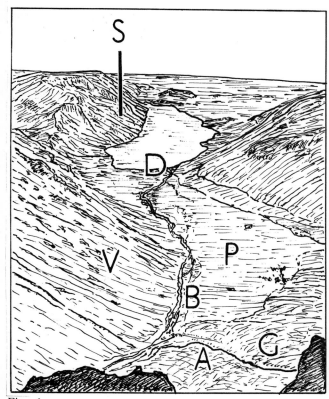

Fig. 162.

Steeply sloping screes (S) of angular, frost-shattered blocks and smaller weathered debris extend down to, and below, water level. The plain (P) shows the extent of alluvial infilling at the head of the lake—still continuing at the delta (D). Notice other small deltas along the lakeside. The patchwork of cultivation shows the fertility of the alluvium. Stream A, incised in glacial deposits (G), joins the braided river B below the slopes of volcanic rocks (V), which show channels of post-glacial run-off. Moraine at the far end of the lake helps to raise the water level.

Fig. 163. Wastwater, in the Lake District, occupies a glacially over-deepened valley. The water surface is 200 feet above sea-level, but its deepest part is 50 feet below sea-level.

The Effects of Ice on Hard Level Surfaces

The high Norwegian fjeld surfaces are the upper, level parts of plateaux formed of very old resistant rocks, worn down and then uplifted. Ice sheets have entirely covered most of the upland areas. The movement of the ice over flat surfaces scooped hollows in weaker places, and on retreat left much debris behind. Here the water-filled hollows show up as small ponds on the once glaciated fjeld; just as on a wider scale a large number of shallow lakes occupy much of the surface of the hard Finnish and Canadian Shields.

After the retreat of the main ice sheets, ice would still form in, and occupy hollows on, the higher parts of the uplands, as in the background. Here there are the remains of shallow corries, still bearing some snow and ice, and from these glacial tongues once extended out onto the high flat surface. They are separated by low arêtes.

Notice the many tiny stones, some from recent weathering, others (erratics) carried and left by moving ice (p. 100).

Fig. 164. The high flat fjeld surface at Sygnefell in Norway. Here, at about 4,600 feet above sea-level, are numerous ice-scooped, water-filled hollows, with a variety of stony debris on the smooth surfaces between. Scale is not easy to assess, but the mountain rises to 6,500 feet.

Lowland Glaciation
Erosion

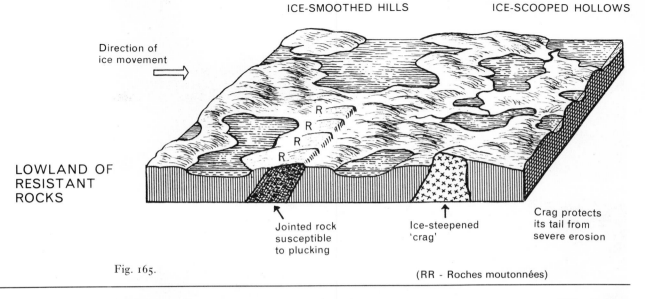

ICE-SMOOTHED HILLS   ICE-SCOOPED HOLLOWS

Direction of
ice movement

LOWLAND OF
RESISTANT
ROCKS

Jointed rock
susceptible
to plucking

Ice-steepened
'crag'

Crag protects
its tail from
severe erosion

Fig. 165.

(RR - Roches moutonnées)

The Actions of Ice Sheets

The encroachment and long-continued movements of massive ice-sheets over a countryside, as with mountain glaciers, caused, and still cause in the case of Antarctica and Greenland, a great deal of erosion; although, compared with most glaciers, the rate of movement of the ice mass is much slower. The effects on the ground, however, vary with the structure and topography, depth of freezing, and position relative to the source of the ice.

The amount of material removed, transported, and deposited also varies, the moraine left as the ice-sheets slowly retreat is that accumulated at the ice face over a long period of time, so that the glacial material covering some lowlands is of the order of hundreds of feet thick.

The Effects on Resistant Rocks

Some parts of the world have extensive areas of old hard rocks which have been worn to a low relief (peneplaned) long ago, and so are particularly resistant to further erosion. The old shield areas of Canada and Finland are of this nature, and were both covered by thick ice-sheets at various periods in the last half-million years (p. 101).

The result has been that low hills were smoothed and rounded. Low rocky outcrops that were resistant and jointed were particularly vulnerable to erosion, being subjected to abrasion by the ice which, armed with sharp rock fragments, overrode and smoothed them. They were also plucked on the down-stream side by ice which froze to the rock and dragged whole blocks away at the joints (Figs. 165 and 169). Such low rocks are known as *roches moutonnées.*

Elsewhere, the gouging action has left hollows in less resistant places, which have subsequently filled with water. Such lake-covered lowlands are typical of the shield areas, where the occasional morainic deposits also interfere with the drainage. These effects, perhaps less dramatically, may be seen on other hard surfaces, on both glaciated lowlands and level uplands, such as the remnants of the dissected plateaux of the Scottish Highlands and Norwegian fjeld seen in Fig. 164.

Outstanding crags, such as volcanic puys (p. 108), have been steepened on those slopes which faced the moving ice; but they tended to protect softer rocks behind, which have remained as a long 'tail'—c.f. the *crag and tail* in Fig. 165. Scratches on the rocks themselves help to indicate the direction of movement of former ice-sheets.

Recent work in Antarctica confirms that the great ice-sheets considerably modify the underlying surfaces. But it is important to realise that they did not *create* the overall landforms of the great shield areas, or of the glaciated tablelands: these had acquired their almost level surfaces by denudation long ago.

Ice Erosion

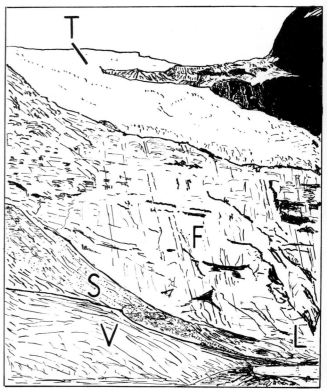

Fig. 167.

T—A tongue of ice represents the surviving part of an ice-mass which once slid downwards to the valley below.

F—The face of the slope shows the effects of abrasion and plucking by the ice.

S—The lower slopes have massive screes, which in parts (V) bear a dense vegetation, mostly of conifers.

L—A lake occupies a portion of the main valley, partly fed by streams coursing down the hillsides.

Fig. 166. The rock face, once covered by a more extensive glacier, shows the effects which moving ice can have on the most resistant surfaces, whether on valley sides or lowlands.

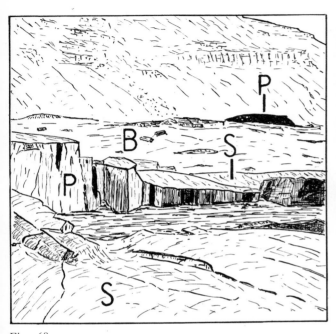

Fig. 168.

Once, ice formed in the joints and bedding planes, and in cracks which were partly created by the weight of the ice-mass itself. As the ice slowly moved forward, whole slabs of rock were detached.

The process was often repeated, and new steep faces were exposed as each block was plucked away by the moving ice (P—plucked faces; B—detached blocks).

The process whereby the rock surface is scratched and smoothed by debris frozen in the ice is called 'abrasion': the finer materials embedded in the ice act almost like a sand-paper, as the smoothness of the surfaces S testify.

Fig. 169. Ice-plucked *roches moutonnées* at the foot of Snowdon, showing the contrast between the smooth rock-scratched surfaces (S) and the sheer faces exposed where blocks have been detached from the parent rock.

Lowland Glaciation
Deposition

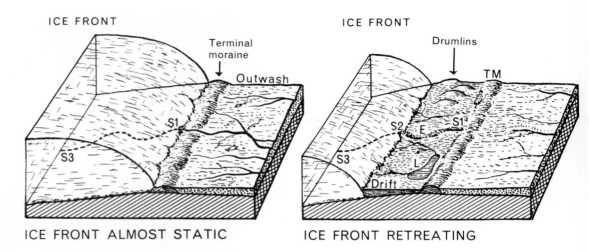

Fig. 170. The accumulation of deposits in front of the ice.

Deposition by Ice Sheets

The morainic material worn from the landscape and transported by the ice-sheets is one of the most common features of glaciated lowlands today. It lies in a thick *drift* over many areas, and often consists of rocks crushed and worn into such a fine powder that they form thick clayey deposits, usually with boulders of various size embedded in them. This material is called *boulder clay*.

But not all glacially deposited material is boulder clay, nor is it always fertile. The sifting effect of melt-water often leaves stretches of gravelly and sandy deposits, and much outwash material is of this nature.

These layers of moraine are left behind as the front of the ice retreats across the lowlands under warmer conditions. But often there are outstanding ridges and hills above the general level of the undulating drift.

Fig. 170 shows where part of the front of an ice-sheet has remained for a considerable period. As the ice melts, leaving the rock debris it has carried, more ice is moving forward and adding to the terminal moraine. The latter may stretch for miles across the countryside as a thick ridge, scores of feet in height, lying, of course, parallel to the ice front.

As, under warmer conditions, the ice front slowly retreats, its moraine is left as a mantle on the ice-eroded lowland. Scattered boulders may be found, some small, some as large as a house, brought by the ice and left on the lowland, perhaps hundreds of miles from their parent rock. These are known as *erratics*, or *erratic blocks* when massive.

In front of the ice-sheet the melt-water forms an outwash plain in advance of the terminal moraine; and, of course, the drainage in front of a retreating ice-sheet is impeded, and wandering water channels and lakes cover the surface. After the ice has gone, some of the moraine-blocked hollows still hold lakes (L). Sometimes the drift has been deposited in rounded hummocks up to several hundred feet high, each with its long axis in the direction of ice movement. These mounds are known as *drumlins*, (D).

Water-sorted Deposits

The great volume of ice-melt water carries fine particles forward, and leaves water-sorted sands and gravels over the adjacent parts of the out-wash plain. There is also much water beneath an ice-sheet, and, even beneath such a great mass of ice, this may flow in stream channels. Such a stream is shown diagrammatically in Fig. 170 by the course S_1 to S_3.

Where the stream pours out from the ice face, the water-sorted, and often rounded, pebbly material builds up. As the ice-front retreats, Fig. 170 B, the stream outlet builds up successive deposits, which come to have the form of a long winding ridge S_1 to S_2, known as an *esker*. These

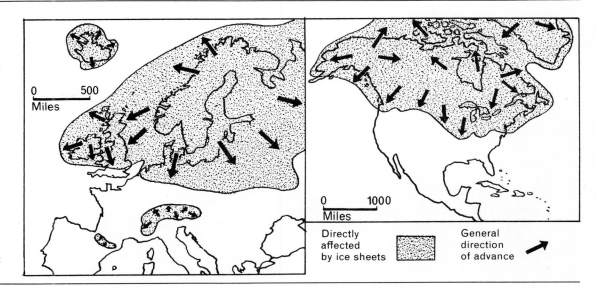

Fig. 171. The limits of maximum glaciation in north-west Europe and North America.

Directly affected by ice sheets

General direction of advance

may stand out in a post-glacial landscape as high sinuous ridges, perhaps divided into sections, but nevertheless characteristic of countryside which once bore the weight of ice-sheets.

The melt-water may also leave irregular patches of water-sorted material, known as *kames*, which lie parallel to the ice face.

Quickly retreating ice may leave no obvious terminal moraines, but just glacial drift, with per- haps, originally, blocks of unmelted ice. These melting blocks may form hollows, or *kettle holes*, which later hold small lakes.

The Extent of Glaciation

Ice-sheets, thousands of feet thick still cover most of Greenland and Antarctica. During the last 600,000 years, ice-sheets have advanced and re- treated four times over much of the area shown in Fig. 171, which shows the limits of maximum glaciation. The effects of glaciation are to be seen well in advance of these limits, however (p. 104).

The maps show the general directions of advance of the ice, e.g. away from such regions of accumula- tion as central Scandinavia. Apart from these, there were also locally thick ice-caps from which ice advanced over the adjoining lowlands. In the British Isles, for example, ice moved from centres in the Scottish Highlands, north Wales, and northern Ireland, as well as advancing to eastern Britain from Scandinavia. As conditions became warmer, local ice-caps remained for a time, as well as many individual mountain glaciers.

Separate glacial centres existed in the regions of

the Alps and Pyrenees, where, today, valley glaciers remain in high mountains.

The results of glaciation in any locality are best appreciated if the positions of the local ice caps at the time of maximum glaciation are known. In Britain, for instance, uplands completely covered by ice now reveal the smoothing and plucking effects usually associated with ice-sheets, as in Fig. 164; while adjacent valleys may have been affected only by individual tongues of glacier ice moving from the ice caps. Ice certainly never provided a uniform cover over the areas seen in Fig. 171.

101

Glacial Erosion

Fig. 172. *Roches moutonnées* near Rydal. Many of the glacially-formed features become part of the general landscape, covered with vegetation and perhaps not immediately obvious as such. The origin of rocky ice-eroded projections is, however, usually more obvious than that of the mounds of deposition (p. 100).

Fig. 173.

Though their appearance is now green, these are rocky projections, with bare exposures at many places on their surface. The nearer face of the large mound shows marked plucking at P, and many of the detached blocks are sheer sided.

This is one of a number of similar mounds, each with a relatively gentle slope on the far side.

The name 'roche moutonnée' was applied long ago to such features, which were thought to bear a general resemblance to the *moutonnées*, or sheepskin wigs, then in fashion.

Glacial Deposition

Fig. 174.

Fig. 175. These cliffs near Cromer are of thick, loose glacial deposits, with a high proportion of chalky particles, flints, and lumps of chalk mixed with silts, sands and gravels. The sea rapidly erodes this soft material and the debris tends to drift along the shore; so that man uses artificial means of preventing its removal and protecting the cliffs.

The cliffs reveal thick deposits which overlie much of the lowlands of eastern England, and are elsewhere revealed in cuttings or open-cast workings (as near brickworks on the Oxford Clay).

The steepness of the lower slopes (L) shows that material is rapidly being removed, and though the upper parts (U) slip and slump downwards (S), their angle is not continued to the shoreline. Protective groynes, such as G, help to check the removal of the beach material, and so lessen the force of the wave attack (p. 124); but nevertheless there is still severe erosion. Vegetation with spreading roots helps to prevent the loose glacial deposits from slipping, and so also checks erosion.

103

In Advance of the Ice

Fig. 176. Natural drainage is prevented by the ice-sheet, and water overspills from the resulting lake through a gap in the escarpment.

Peri-Glacial Features

The term describes those features in advance of the edge (*peri*meter) of the ice-sheets: regions not actually covered by ice, but affected by melt-water or later, perhaps, by wind-borne dust derived from glacial debris. Among these are, of course, the badly drained outwash plains (Fig. 170). In advance of the present northern ice-sheets, tundra conditions exist, as they did further south during the period of maximum glaciation—a landscape of moist soils and watery hollows, of mosses and lichens, short grasses and tiny herbs—a stony landscape, bright green or flower-covered in early summer, not unlike that in Fig. 178.

Much of Britain must have been like this at times during the Ice Ages. The sub-soil does not fully thaw out during the summer, so that below a certain depth *permafrost* exists, and above it the water-table is high.

Some of England's broad valleys in the southern chalk downs, which were not directly glaciated, may have been cut by the plentiful surface water of those periods (Fig. 55).

Ice-Blocked Lakes

There is much evidence that during the Ice Ages normal drainage was often blocked by tongues of ice, and the melt-water thus ponded back formed lakes. The excess water was apt to spill through valleys, which were widened and deepened. Present rivers may follow old overflow courses, and streams occupy valleys much too big for them to have formed themselves. Sometimes the direction of flow of a whole river system may have been changed by such blockage. The Yorkshire Derwent and several Cotswold streams provide examples of such diversion through old overspill channels.

Loess from Moraine

Fine dust, carried by winds far from the drying morainic material left by the ice, may settle and build up a deep, loose, potentially fertile cover, known as *loess*. In north-western Europe such loess areas, derived from drying moraines of recent glacial advances, lie in a belt from northern Germany to north-eastern France, and provide very fertile soils.

Depression by Ice Caps

The weight of a huge ice-cap can cause depression of part of the earth's crust during an Ice Age. The Scandinavian ice-caps depressed the land considerably, the Scottish ones less. After an Ice Age a recovery of level occurs, usually in stages. Such vertical movements are known as *isostatic* adjustments. The study of their extent is complicated by changes in sea level due to ice-cap formation and then melting, for an isostatic uplift may be less apparent if there is also a general rise in sea-level.

Where Moving Ice Meets the Sea

Icebergs and Pack Ice

Where ice sheets meet the sea, the forward movement of the ice continues and great masses break off to form icebergs, which float away with a large proportion submerged (nine-tenths, if the ice were pure—but, in fact, varying according to the amount of trapped air and rock debris). The break-away process is known as 'calving'.

In Fig. 177 masses of drift ice and a certain amount of close pack ice are also seen in the fiord. Notice, on the land area, the many corries, and evidence of a shrinking ice cover—in the nearer corries ice is sparse or absent, though further inland ice-tongues extend towards the main ice sheet. The smoothness of the foreground slopes also suggest earlier, more extensive glaciation. Notice also the long line of medial moraine, clearly visible where the ice meets the inlet.

Fig. 177. At the head of a deep inlet in the coast of East Greenland pack ice is forming offshore, and icebergs are calved by huge glaciers descending slowly to the sea from the more continuous and thick ice cover inland.

Glacial Erosion and Deposition

Fig. 178. A summer scene in eastern Iceland. Cultivation is limited; and the sod roofing of the byres (B) and the steep-pitched roofs of the houses are testaments to the cold, snowy winters. The green summer appearance, given by grasses and mosses, is typical of these latitudes.

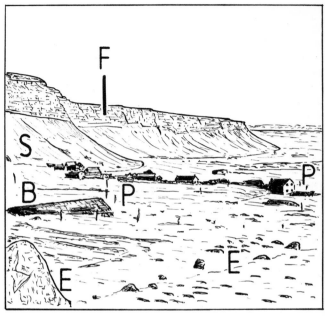

Fig. 179.

The upper slopes, or free-face (F), show the effects of weathering, and the rock debris from the bare surface collects to form the scree slopes (S) beneath; these lie at a very uniform 'angle of repose'.

The lowland has, in former times, been heavily glaciated and erratic blocks (E) lie scattered over the rocky ice-eroded surface. The whole scene, therefore, shows processes both of wearing away and of accumulation—by weathering and gravity, and by glacial actions.

The larger poles (P) are used for drying hay—pointing to the dampness of the sunny summer months which follow the long snowy winters.

Transport and Deposition by Ice

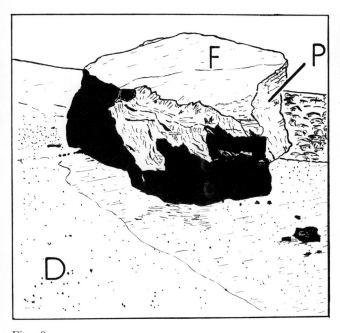

Fig. 180.

Fig. 181. An erratic block on a melting ice surface in a glaciated valley in eastern Iceland. This is being abandoned fairly close to the source of the ice; but extensive retreating ice-sheets can leave stranded blocks hundreds of miles from their place of origin.

Rocks may be carried forward on the surface of the ice, or may become embedded within its mass. In each case they are ultimately left stranded when the ice as a whole melts.

The sides of this erratic block show plucking (P); notice also the fracture (F). Strong cold winds sweep down this valley and the surface of the ice becomes littered also with fine wind-borne rock debris (D). Even smaller particles may be carried by the wind from drying morainic deposits, and may sometimes build up deposits of 'loess' on a far distant surface.

Part V Vulcanicity

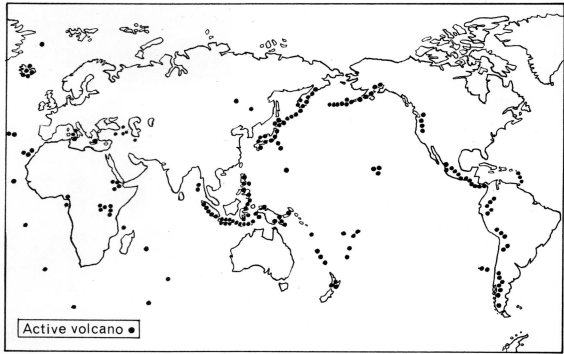

Active volcano ●

Fig. 182. The distribution of large active volcanoes. There is also volcanic activity in parts of Antarctica not shown on the map.

Landscape Features of Volcanic Origin

In many landscapes a number of features owe their form to past or present volcanic action—some, like the cones of Figs. 188 and 190, are easily recognisable as such; others, like the end products of weathering and erosion on such cones may, as residual stumps, or *puys*, be less easy to identify. In some places solidified lava flows may wind across the landscape; in others the ancient outpourings may only be revealed sandwiched between the older and newer rocks; elsewhere the surface rocks themselves may be made up of thick layers of debris accumulated from long-continued volcanic eruptions.

Volcanoes

Their Distribution

Fig. 182 shows the distribution of active volcanoes in the world (although it is difficult to define

'active'—as some have long periods of quiescence, while others erupt frequently).

A large proportion are situated in, or close to, the zones of recent mountain building—from the Alps and Himalayas to Indonesia, and especially in the regions of recent mountain formation about the Pacific, forming a so-called 'girdle of fire'. In these zones earthquake activity is also relatively frequent. Another association is with the trends of the great rifts in the earth's surface—as shown by volcanic activity near the great African rift valleys and the mid-oceanic ridges.

Their Nature

Volcanoes of the 'ash cone and crater' type have a central 'pipe' through which the hot gases and molten lavas emerge; though sometimes the lavas issue through secondary vents on the slopes of the main volcanic cone.

The ash, or cinder, cone is built up as the materials thrown out come to rest—most falling near the vent, and sloping out at the angle of repose of the fragments.

Some flows are composite ones, being built partly of ash and partly of flows of lava issuing from near the base of the volcano.

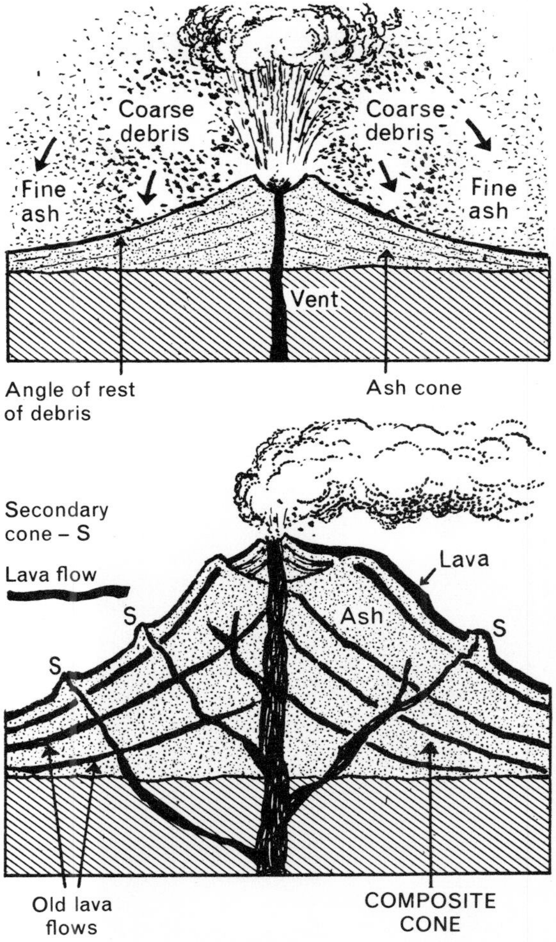

The larger particles thrown out during eruptions fall back near the crater. The finer ones may be carried a long way on the winds. When deposits build up and harden into thick layers, they are known as volcanic *tuff*.

Gases bubbling through molten lava make it frothy, so that on ejection it solidifies into a light *pumice*.

Calderas

After a cone has been quiescent for some time, a violent eruption may blow out the solidified 'plug' of lava and also much of the top of the cone. The cavity which remains, enclosed by a rim of volcanic material, is known as a *caldera*. But many large calderas have a form which suggest that explosion was followed by the collapse of the whole central structure of the volcano and subsidence below the centre. *Crater lakes* (Fig. 191) may

Fig. 183. A cone of ash; and a composite cone with ash and lava flows intermingled.

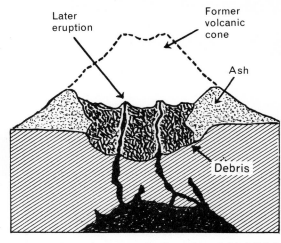

Fig. 184. Secondary cones rise from the subsided debris within a caldera.

occupy the resulting cavity, some of them many miles across. Secondary cones often rise above the floor of the caldera, or stand out as islands in the lakes.

Lava Flows

Lavas usually emerge from volcanic vents at between 900°–1,200°C. They may flow freely for long distances, cooling and solidifying as they do.

The ease with which they flow depends on their mobility. In general, those which contain much silica (*acidic lavas*) tend to be viscous and solidify rapidly, and so do not flow so far. Those with less silica, and rich in iron and magnesium, (*basic lavas*) tend to flow readily and spread more widely. The latter include the basic rocks shown in Figs. 195–200, where the solidification of successive flows has built up a variety of land forms. In general, it is the basic lavas which tend, by weathering, to produce fertile soils.

109

Volcanoes and Volcanic Flows

Fig. 185. A fairly recent cinder cone rises from the savannahs of northern Tanzania, not far from Mt. Kilimanjaro. The whole surface is covered with the remains of successive volcanic out-pourings.

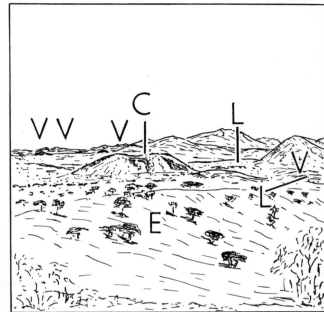

Fig. 186.

In some parts of the world, as here in East Africa, volcanic materials, erupted through vents and fissures, cover a very large part of the landscape, and may extend over thousands of square miles of the surface. In this region volcanic activity has occurred over tens of millions of years, up to recent times. In Fig. 185, we see a cinder cone C, bearing a radial pattern of drainage (p. 44), and also numerous volcanic hills (VV) of varying age and dissection. Lava flows form ridges on the surface, and in the foreground the edge E is that of an extensive flow—and not, as might appear, that of a caldera (p. 109), the view-point being from the top of another outstanding cone.

Successive Eruptions

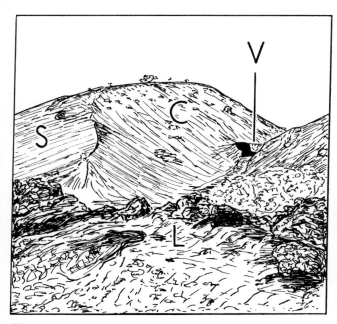

Fig. 187.

Fig. 188. The central part of a recent volcano in the Tsavo savannahs of southern Kenya, with vegetation beginning to establish itself on the ash and on the solidified lava.

The slope S is that of the accumulation of ash built up by the original volcanic activity. The volcano became dormant, but a later eruption destroyed the centre of the cone, with its solidified plug, and cinder and ash fell into the crater C. A further, small, relatively recent eruption has occurred, and lava pouring from the vent V formed a moving, fiery wall, which has solidified, as seen in the foreground at L.

Already plants have established themselves on the ash of the cone and on the lava itself.

Vulcanicity

INTRUSIVE DYKES

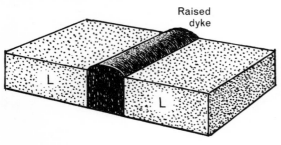

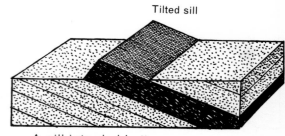

L – Less resistant ⎱ Than the
M – More resistant ⎰ intrusive rock

A sill intruded between
the bedding planes

Fig. 189. Intrusive rocks exposed by denudation.

Eruptions through Fissures

Very extensive flows of basic lavas, especially of those which solidify to form the dark, fine-grained *basalt*, are apt to emerge, through fissures, without any explosive activity. Great thicknesses of basalt have been extruded and built up by individual flows, and in many parts of the earth cover hundreds of square miles of the surface: on the Deccan plateau in India, on the intermontane plateau of the Columbia-Snake River plateau region of the U.S.A., and elsewhere.

As the basalt sheets cool they may contract to form six-sided columns—seen in the flows in Fig. 197.

Associated Features

Some volcanoes, though not erupting for long periods, have remained active in that their craters are hot, though emitting only steam and sulphurous gases; they are then known as *solfatara*. *Hot springs*

and *geysers* (Fig. 49) also occur in volcanically active areas, or in some regions of past activity.

Intrusive Forms

So far the features described involve the extrusion of volcanic materials through vents or fissures onto the surface.

In some cases the molten magma does not flow out as lava, but is forced to intrude into fissures below the surface, or finds weaknesses between bedding planes, where it cools and hardens.

Magma solidifying in a vertical fissure can produce a *dyke*, which may be revealed when the rocks above are worn away. Sometimes, as seen in Fig. 189, it may form a long ridge, sometimes a trench.

Intrusive lavas may solidify, sometimes between bedding planes, as thick horizontal layers, and later become exposed, perhaps after earth movements have tilted them and erosion has laid bare their edge. A layer of this type, horizontal or tilted

is known as a *sill*. The Great Whin Sill in Northumberland (Figs. 195 and 196) is exposed in this way, and carries such defensive features as Hadrian's Wall and Bamburgh Castle.

Other intrusions also occur, though not necessarily giving such regular features. The resistant solidified magma of the vents of old volcanoes often remain as outstanding steep-sided plugs, or *puys*, sometimes used as defensive sites, like those of Auvergne in central France, or landmarks such as Captain Cook's Glasshouse Mountains, north of Brisbane.

Some ancient intrusive rocks which were once deep seated masses *(batholiths)* have become exposed by the erosion of the rocks which covered them—like the granites which now form the core of the Wicklow Mountains in Ireland, and those of Dartmoor. These slowly cooled rocks, with their large crystals, are very different from the dark iron-rich rocks of Figs. 195–200—as indicated on p. 1.

Volcanic Activity Shapes the Landscape

Mt. Ngauruhoe is one of three huge volcanoes in the central part of the North Island of New Zealand, a region of igneous activity which includes eruptions, solfatara, hot springs, and geysers (p. 28).

A vast quantity of molten magma has been released, building up the outstanding Volcanic Plateau, which bears thick coverings of ejected lavas and ash. This is one of the world's youngest and largest accumulations of acid volcanic rocks, covering more than 10,000 square miles.

Fig. 190 shows the cone, from which spectacular eruptions still take place, and below it a broken surface of solidified lava flows. Vegetation often establishes itself quite rapidly on recent flows (Fig. 188), and here in the foreground is an extensive covering of coarse tussock grasses.

The volcanic slopes are snow-covered, for Ngauruhoe rises to over 7,500 feet, and nearby Ruapehu to over 9,000 feet.

Fig. 190. The cone of the volcano Mt. Ngauruhoe in the Tongariro National Park on the Volcanic Plateau in the centre of the North Island of New Zealand.

Crater Lake and a Secondary Volcano

Fig. 191. Lago di Vico, north of Rome, lies within a great volcanic caldera, which contains a large secondary cone (V). The lake has shrunk in recent times, leaving a flat alluvial floor (A), very suitable for growing fruit and grain crops.

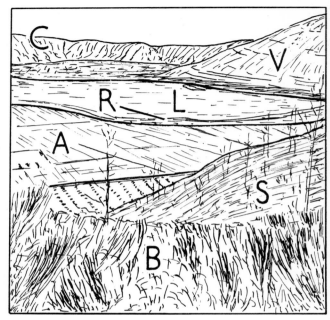

Fig. 192.

The crater is seen from part of its rim, whose ash slopes (S) support only light coppice and broom on its dry acidic soils. The steep slopes are deeply gullied.

The crater lake (L) was once much more extensive, and in the shallow water at the edge of the shrinking lake lines of rushes (R) can be seen. The old lake bed remains as fertile, sheltered farmland, cultivated on all sides of the present lake.

Beyond can be seen the far walls of this large caldera (C), also much gullied and covered mainly with broom and scrub woodland.

A Composite Volcanic Mass

Fig. 193.

Fig. 194. Kibo, one of the two main volcanic heights of the great mass of Mt. Kilimanjaro, standing at over 19,000 ft., is seen from the saddle extending from the neighbouring peak, Mawenzi, 7 miles distant. The scenery shows the combined effects of eruption, weathering, erosion, and deposition.

The main crater, surrounded by snow, lies within the composite mass of cinder and lava, C, whose eroded slopes rise to the highest point in Africa. Flows of lava can be seen on the flanks, especially at F. In the middle distance, ridges have built up from the secondary vents at V. In the foreground are boulders (B) of considerable size, flung out during eruptions; coarse grasses grow between, even at this height. To the right, the more gentle slope is covered with fine material (A) washed down from the steeper ashy slopes above.

115

Intrusive Rocks   Sill Formation

Dolerite is the most common basic rock of igneous origin found in intrusive sills and dykes.

It forms the tilted Whin Sill, seen in Figs. 195 and 196, created by molten matter injected into the rocks sometime after they were formed; (it is *not* sandwiched between earlier and later rocks). From some deeper source it found, and forced its way into, weak places between beds, where it solidified. The slow rate of cooling results in crystals which are larger than those formed in basalt (p. 2).

In places, the tilted edge of the dolerite Whin Sill forms a low north-facing escarpment, as in those stretches which bear Hadrian's Wall.

Elsewhere it is found folded and arched together with the Carboniferous strata, again looking, deceptively, as though it had been bedded along with those rocks.

Fig. 195. The Whin Sill dolerite, lying above folded, jointed Carboniferous Limestone, near Alnwick. Here, at Cullernose Point, it forms part of the coast of northern Northumberland: the dark vertical cliffs are seen in the background. The Sill runs for many miles across northeast England to the Scottish border.

The Great Whin Sill

The rock on which the castle stands is not lava which has poured out of surface vents, but is, as indicated, the dolerite which has solidified as a sill injected into rocks of the Carboniferous series.

In many places there are signs that the molten rock changes the form of the Carboniferous layers in contact with it, both above and below (a metamorphic change, p. 5). This fact has enabled men to establish its origin as a sill.

The rock seen in Figs. 195 and 196 has a columnar appearance, though not as pronounced as in the hexagonal basalt columns shown in Fig. 197.

Fig. 196. Bamburgh Castle in Northumberland stands astride the intrusive Great Whin Sill, which divides successive beds of Carboniferous rocks. This is the eastern part of the sill in northern Northumberland; its final appearance in the east being in the Farne Islands.

Volcanic Flows

Fig. 198.

The cave, formed in lava flows of different periods, is some 230 feet long. The entrance is flanked by the hexagonal basalt columns, formed by shrinkage when the molten rock cooled at the former surface. Basalt, being a basic lava, flows quite readily, in contrast to the more acidic lavas. The photograph clearly shows the difference in texture between the basalt and the lava flows which solidified above it (L).

Fig. 197. The entrance to Fingal's Cave on the island of Staffa, west of Mull in Argyllshire. Here successive flows of lava accumulated during the Alpine mountain building period, and form the present low, flat island.

Volcanic Flows

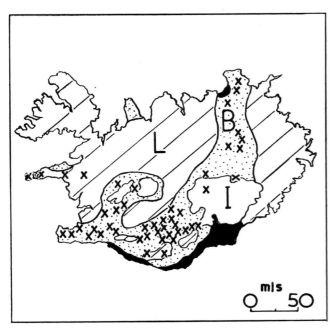

Fig. 199. Iceland—The surface rocks.

Fig. 200. Gothafoss in northern Iceland, where the river is fed by rains and snow melt, and the waters cascade over a series of falls formed in lava flows of varying age.

Iceland is entirely built up of volcanic rocks, although the areas shaded black in Fig. 199 have thicknesses of alluvial material derived from the volcanic accumulations and spread by flood waters. Much of the surface, as in Fig. 200, is of dark basaltic lavas (L), which have poured from numerous fissures and solidified. In the belt B (Fig. 199) recent outflows overlie the Tertiary ones. Here there are also volcanoes (x), hot springs and geysers, and eruptions which occur even beneath the remaining ice-caps (I).

Many rushing torrents have cut deep into the lava beds. Some falls are caused by varying rock resistance, while others are due to the frequent faulting, and to knickpoints (p. 64) resulting from the consequent changes in level.

Part VI Oceans, Shores, and Coasts

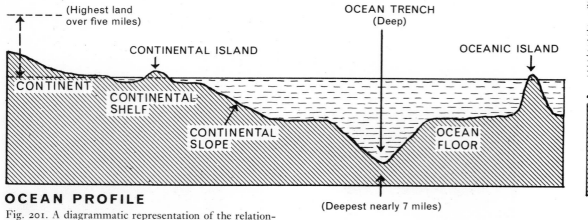

OCEAN PROFILE

Fig. 201. A diagrammatic representation of the relationship between various continental and oceanic features.

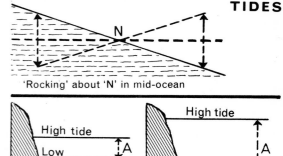

'Rocking' about 'N' in mid-ocean

NEAP TIDE   SPRING TIDE

A – 'Amplitude' or 'Range'

Ocean Profile

At the outer limit of a continental landmass the submerged part of the continent itself, known as the *continental shelf*, from which various islands project, falls away down the *continental slope* of fairly gentle gradient to the much deeper ocean floor.

In some oceans submarine plateaux rise above the general level of the ocean floor; in others, notably in the Atlantic, a ridge rises in mid-ocean, and parts of this may project in the form of oceanic islands. In the Atlantic, the ridge is associated with volcanic activity, and in places volcanic islands, such as Iceland and the Azores mark the line of this remarkably continuous mid-oceanic feature.

In other parts of the oceans, usually bordering zones of recent mountain building, there are deep trenches; and though the descent to these trenches is down surprisingly gentle inclines, those off eastern Asia slope down to depths of almost seven miles.

Movements of Ocean Waters

The gravitational attractions of sun and moon set up a rocking motion in the main ocean areas. The effect is greatest when the sun, moon, and earth are 'in line', and least when the attractive forces of the sun and moon are at right-angles to one another.

Fig. 202 shows the resultant alternations of high and low tides and variation in amplitude. As the earth rotates, each meridian comes into a position of high tide twice, and low tide twice, every 24 hours 52 minutes.

The lower diagrams show how the tidal variations relate to the phases of the moon. To an observer on earth the large amplitude of the spring tides occurs at the time of new moon and full moon; while the low tidal ranges of the neap tides occur when there is a half moon. The highest spring tides of all occur at the equinoxes.

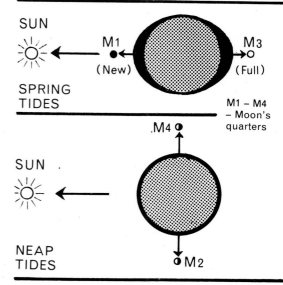

Fig. 202. High water banked up at spring tides, and more evenly spread out at neap tides.

Ocean Circulation

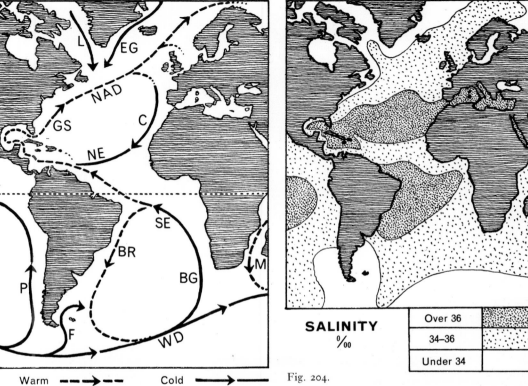

Fig. 203. Currents:

GS — Gulf Stream
L — Labrador
EG — East Greenland
NAD — North Atlantic Drift
C — Canaries
NE — North Equatorial
BG — Benguela
BR — Brazil
P — Peru
SE — South Equatorial
WD — Wind Drift
M — Mozambique
F — Falkland

Warm ---►--- Cold ——►——

SALINITY ‰

Over 36	
34–36	
Under 34	

Fig. 204.

Surface Currents

These are largely set in motion by the prevailing winds, and deflected by the land-masses, so that there is a regular pattern of continuous circulation. Surface water, warmed in the tropics, may flow to a higher latitude as a warm current; while water flowing from cooler latitudes forms a relatively cold current compared with the seas to which it flows.

Notice in Fig. 203 the relationships of currents to prevailing Westerlies and Trades, deflections by the continents, and the return of waters after circulation in the Arctic. Such circulation occurs in other oceans, though the monsoonal changes in wind direction cause seasonal changes of flow in the northern Indian Ocean.

Vertical movements, caused by density differences, also occur. Cold water tends to sink beneath warm, and salt beneath fresh. Air moving the surface water away from a coast may also allow cooler water to well up from below.

Salinity (Saltiness)

The seas receive salts from rivers; and chemical actions within the oceans add or remove salts.

Evaporation by wind and the sun's heat causes salt concentration in surface water, whereas much rainfall, fresh river water, and ice-melt dilute ocean waters.

Ocean salinity in the hot Trade Wind belts may be over 36‰, compared with only 7‰ in the cool, river-fed Baltic Sea, and nearly 240‰ in the enclosed Dead Sea, where salts brought by the Jordan evaporate in desert conditions. Seas whose waters cannot mix freely with ocean water generally differ in surface salinity from the open ocean.

121

Salinity

Fig. 205. Salt pans established at the entrance to a broad bay on the dry south-western coast of Puerto Rico, where the north-east Trades are off-shore. Salt, seen piled up across the inlet, has been formed from the sea-water evaporating within the shallow pans.

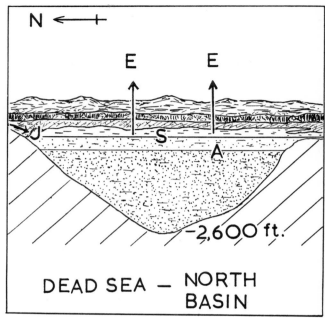

Fig. 206. Evaporation causing surface salinity to approach 240‰.

The Dead Sea lies in a rift valley, its surface (S) about 1,290 feet below sea level. The deep north basin is joined by a shallow channel to the much less deep southern basin.

The River Jordan (J) contributes both water and dissolved salts at the north end of the lake. In the hot, very dry climate, the rate of evaporation equals that of the water contributed (E—loss by evaporation).

Much gypsum (calcium sulphate), in the form of tiny crystals, and calcium carbonate, are precipitated in the upper waters. A dense, salty layer (SA), some 130 feet deep, lies above even denser, still, bottom water (below A). The deepest parts are about 2,600 feet below sea-level. Changes in level have left thick salt deposits exposed, and today salt crusts are formed where waves wash the shores: a commodity of considerable economic value.

Coastal Erosion

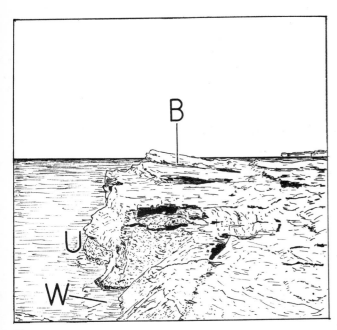

Fig. 207.

Fig. 208. In Malta the action of waves and salt water spray on the gently tilted limestones are rapidly destroying the coastline, by undercutting the cliffs, widening joints, and dissolving the rock itself. The upper limestone shows staining from the red soil which once covered the surface.

The vulnerability of exposed limestone rocks is described in some detail on pp. 18-26.

Here we see the results of the combination of the physical force of the waves, the chemical action of sea water, and the work of 'sub-aerial' processes (p. 12) which affect any rocks exposed to the atmosphere.

Notice the widening between the almost horizontal bedding planes (B), the opened joints, and the exposed solution hollows within the rock. Below, the wave action has physically undercut the cliff face (U), and traces of the wave-cut platform are visible (W) beneath the water.

Wind-borne spray and rain also affect the cliffs, even where there is little direct wave action, and the whole face shows the irregularities produced by local solution, sometimes called 'rotting'.

The Action of Waves

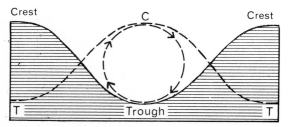

Fig. 209. In the open ocean.

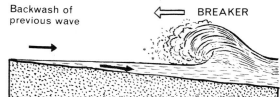

Fig. 210. On the foreshore.

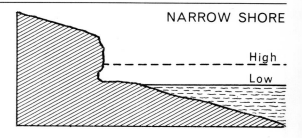

NARROW SHORE

High

Low

LONG SHELVING SHORE

High

Low

Fig. 211. The influence of shore and beach.

The Waves Themselves

The wind sweeping over the sea agitates the surface into the undulations known as waves, and provides the energy which the wave motion (but not the water itself) carries forward, as the crests and troughs move across the ocean. The height of the waves depends on the strength and duration of the wind and on the length of open water (*fetch*) across which the wind blows.

Crests succeed troughs, but the individual water particles simply follow a circular motion, like that shown by the broken line in Fig. 209.

Breaking on the Shore

When the wave advance reaches a shallowing shore, and the depth becomes insufficient for the complete undulation, the top of the wave breaks forward and water carrying beach debris surges up the shore as *swash*, and then falls back as *backwash*.

These actions play a great part in building up and removing beach material; although a return 'under-tow', or undercurrent (Fig. 210), is more effective in the latter process than the backwash.

Waves as Erosive Agents

The thump of waves on a cliff compresses air in the joints and cracks on a rock face, and as the waves fall back the air is allowed to expand. These dual forces help to loosen the rocks and hasten cliff erosion.

Pebbles hurled forward help the destructive action (*corrasion*), and are themselves worn into smaller particles (*attrition*).

The physical force itself is often very great, and waves can exert pressures of more than a ton per square foot.

The effectiveness of waves in causing erosion depends on the energy with which they strike the coast. This energy may be lessened where the waves travel first over a gently sloping shore with much beach material, and they may then only be effective agents of erosion at high tide (Fig. 211). On the other hand, where beach development is slight, the cliffs may be subjected to some wave action at all times.

High winds, local storms, and exceptionally high tides, especially at the equinoxes, tend to cause exaggerated wave action, and the effects on the coast can be great when these act in conjunction.

The Direction of Wave Attack

The effects of wave action depend partly on the angle at which the wave front meets the coast. Fig. 212 shows how waves behave on reaching an indented coastline, and why the wave crests tend to advance in directions which respond to the curves of the bays and headlands.

As the waves move from position H to position G, they encounter first the shallower water opposite the headland and are slowed up. Opposite the bay, the water is deeper to begin with, so that the waves advance into the bay more rapidly. This eventually

Profile of bay
and approaches

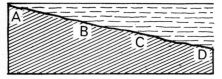

Profile of headland
and approaches

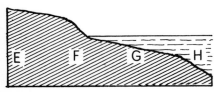

Fig. 212(a). Comparative depths.

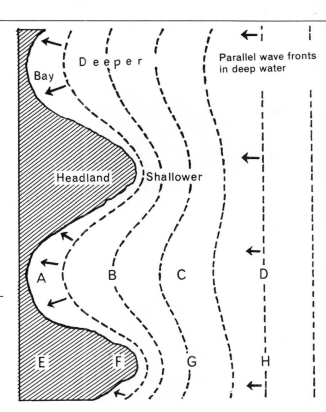

Deeper

Bay

Parallel wave fronts
in deep water

Headland   Shallower

A   B   C   D

E   F   G   H

Fig. 212(b). In deep water the wave fronts are parallel. The retarding influence of shallow water is met first off the headland. This is seen in the profiles on the left, where comparisons may be made of depths at D and H, C and G, with reference to these letters also on the diagram above.

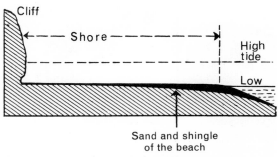

COASTLINE

Cliff

Shore

High
tide

Low

Sand and shingle
of the beach

Fig. 213. Terms applied to coastal features.

means that a swinging effect takes place, making the line of advance of the waves generally parallel to the shore. It also means that the energy of attack on the headlands is more concentrated than on the shores of the bay, where the conditions are less disturbed—so that bays generally offer safer anchorage for shipping as well as shelter from winds.

The winds may, in fact, alter to some extent the direction of advance of the wave front relative to the shoreline. Also, as deposition increases within the bays, they may become less effective anchorages.

Shore, Beach and Coast

These different terms are applied to various parts of the zone in which the land meets the sea, and it is important to distinguish between them (Fig. 213).

The *shore* extends from the sea margin at low tide to the high-water mark. The loose material, which may consist of boulders, shingle, sand, or mud, forms what is known as the *beach*. The term *coast* refers to the boundary of the land itself, and tends to include the features mentioned, with the cliffs and cliff tops, tidal reaches, etc.

The Force of the Waves

In the background is the northernmost part of Exmoor, and in the foreground part of a wide bay in which beach deposits and shingle banks have been built up near the shore. The sea-wall protects the coast, the town, and marshy lowlands from the force of the waves at high tide.

Here the waves advance over deep water in the bay itself and, as they reach shallow water over the pebble banks before the wall, break suddenly and rush forward, like the white wave surge seen in the background.

In the foreground, the force of the breaking wave strikes the sea-wall, hurling a destructive load of pebbles against the face, some of which can be seen lying on the promenade beyond. On this particular occasion, at the next high tide, and during storm conditions, the waves flooded the promenade, leaving great mounds of gravel to be removed from the front.

It is the combination of wave force and the pounding of pebbles and small boulders which is so destructive to an unprotected cliff face.

In Figs. 59 and 244 the deposition along the shores of Porlock Bay, on the far side of this northern extension of Exmoor, gives some idea of the amount of material which may be carried by waves.

Fig. 214. Waves thump against the protective sea-wall at Minehead in Somerset. Beyond lie the pebbles which have been carried forward and thrown against and over the wall.

Coastal Erosion and the Deposition of Beach Material

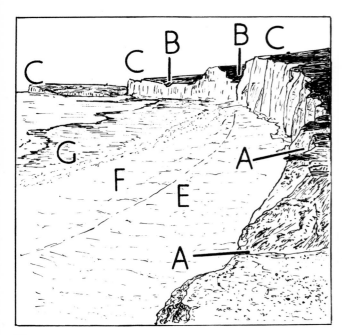

Fig. 215.

Here the chalk as a whole has a very even texture and erosion by the waves has worn back the cliffs to form a remarkably regular profile (CC). The texture of the rock also allows it to form a very steep angle of slope. Beneath is evidence of recent rock falls.

Valleys in the chalk downland have been truncated and left hanging (B). In the foreground the texture changes and weaknesses allow the sea to create deeper inlets (AA).

Beneath, the lower wave-cut platform at G bears little beach material, although dark with patches of weed; but above this the waves have thrown up banks of pebbles, with ridges fairly well defined between E and F. A beach of this kind lessens the severity of wave attack on the cliffs.

Fig. 216. The chalk cliffs of the Sussex coast with a wave-cut platform exposed beneath a well-developed pebble beach. Notice the regularity of cliff retreat, almost as if the face has been planed back mechanically.

Erosion and Coastal Landforms

BEFORE COLLAPSE   **I**

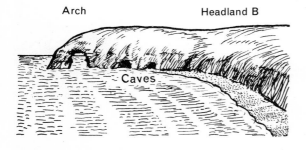

AFTER COLLAPSE   **II**

Fig. 217 (profiles I and II).

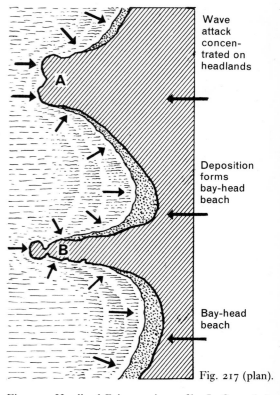

Fig. 217 (plan).

Processes of Erosion

The attack which is concentrated on the exposed headlands usually results in fairly rapid erosion. Joints and other weaknesses are picked out and inlets formed, perhaps with the development of caves. The rapidity of disintegration and retreat of the headland depends on the rock structure as well as on the exposure to wave action.

Fig. 217 shows how caves may join to form arches; and when, in time, collapse occurs the remnant of the headland becomes detached, in the form of a *stack* on a low wave-cut platform, and continues to be reduced by wave action.

The eroded material is transported by tidal flow and by currents, and is apt to be deposited in the bays (p. 140); so that, as the headlands are worn back, the shores within the bays are being extended by beach deposits.

The profiles I and II show the effects of these processes on and near the headland B.

Figs. 219 and 222 also show these processes in action on the chalk cliffs of England's east and south coasts. The action is not, of course, confined to this type of rock, though the less resistant, jointed rocks are obviously most vulnerable.

Fig. 217. Headland B is seen in profile. In Stage I the caves have joined to form an arch. A bay-head beach is building up as eroded material from the cliffs is deposited on the shore. Deposits may also be derived from alluvium brought to the coast by rivers and streams and drifted into the bays.

By Stage II, the collapse of the arch has separated part of the headland from the rest, forming the stack. A new arch has developed from another cave, or pair of caves. Within the bay, the beach has become more extensive.

Fig. 218. Erosion leading to the formation of caves and long inlets.

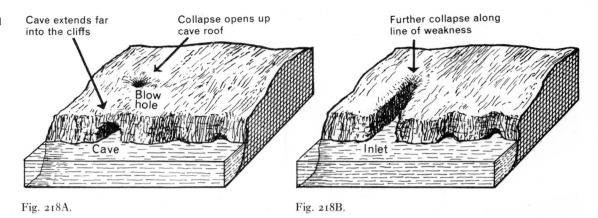

Fig. 218A.

Fig. 218B.

Caves, Blow-Holes and Inlets

As outlined, the sea enlarges joints and other lines of weakness, and extends caves deep into the cliffs. In some cases, far into the rock, the ceiling of a cave collapses, leaving a hole extending down from the cliff-top. The hydraulic action of the water at high tide, compressing air in the rock joints (p. 124) is often responsible for the collapse.

In some places, each time a wave surges through the cave at high tide, spray may shoot up to considerable heights through the opening, which is then known as a 'blow-hole' (Fig. 218A).

Fig. 218B shows that complete collapse along a line of weakness, and the removal by the sea of the debris from the roof, may lead to the formation of a long narrow inlet. There are some fine examples of all these features in the well-jointed Old Red Sandstone cliffs in the far north of Scotland, where an inlet formed in this way is known as a *geo*—pronounced with a hard 'g'.

Weathering and Coastal Features

On all outstanding coastlands, the effects of weathering are as important as they are in inland locations. In addition, sea-cliffs are particularly exposed to winds and corrosive spray which help the disintegration of the surface rocks. Sea-cliffs are often far from regular in appearance. Gravity causes exposed water-saturated strata to slump forward from cliff faces, and the weathered material to build scree slopes. Birds and animals may loosen the rock surfaces and aid these processes.

The Removal of Cliff Debris

One great difference between weathering in inland and coastal locations concerns the after-effects of such actions; for the sea, by its scouring and backwash, may rapidly remove the materials which accumulate at the base of the slopes. Longshore currents and waves oblique to the shore may carry the debris for long distances.

Because of this, the lower rock face lacks protection and remains exposed to erosive action; under-cutting at the base of the cliff may cause fresh falls and so expose new faces higher up the cliffs to weathering.

The removal of debris is seldom a continuous process; and though destructive waves, with a strong backwash, may operate over a period of time, this may be followed by a period during which the waves are mainly constructive and build up materials which protect the cliffs from erosion (p. 133) and so from weathering.

Man may help the processes of cliff destruction by dredging offshore, and so allowing waves to move material from the beaches into deeper water, removing the protection to the base of the cliffs. Fig. 225 shows the opposite processes in operation, lessening the rate of erosion.

Weaknesses Exploited by the Waves

Fig. 219. At Flamborough Head on the Yorkshire coast, thick chalk, with flints, forms almost vertical cliffs, which contrast with the hummocky and slumped glacial drift above and inland of them. Wave action has produced spectacular caves and inlets.

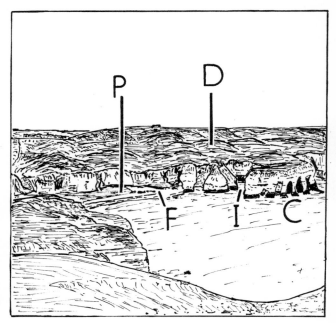

Fig. 220.

The sea has exploited weaknesses in the cliffs, particularly the faults which are common along this part of the coast, and also numerous minor joints, and has formed caves (C) and inlets (I) in the chalk. The marks of wave action can clearly be seen at the base of the cliffs.

At P the cliffs have receded to leave a platform, but there are still signs of undercutting, and cliff falls can be seen at F. As might be expected, this part of the coast also has examples of stacks and blow-holes (pp. 128-9).

Glacial deposits D lie above the cliffs, and are responsible for the hummocky appearance of the surface.

Headland Erosion

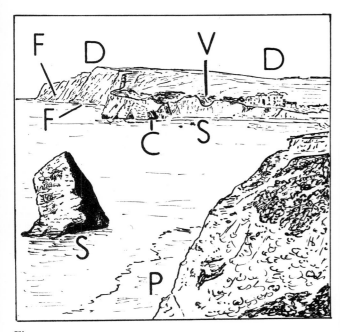

Fig. 221.

Fig. 222. Beyond Freshwater Bay in the Isle of Wight, the smooth profile of the Downs (DD) ends abruptly in magnificent chalk cliffs, cut back by sea erosion. The generally steep slopes are lessened by fallen material (F) at the foot of the cliffs. Those about the bay in the foreground show many features of coastal erosion.

By continuing in the mind's eye the profile of the far headland, we can estimate the extent of the inroads made on the coastlands by marine erosion.

Notice the almost vertical cliffs, and the way in which existing valleys (V) are left hanging as the cliffs retreat.

The middle headland shows the beginnings of cave formation at C. Stacks occur at S. That in the foreground is probably a relic of cliff collapse: notice the flat surface on the landward face and how the once level bedding, discernible in the foreground has been tilted upward by the fall. Part of the platform is visible through the water.

131

The Nature of the Cliffs

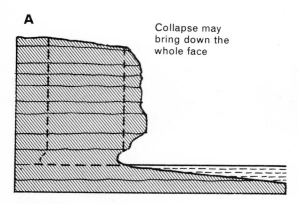

A

Collapse may bring down the whole face

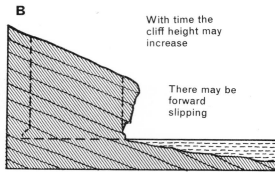

B

With time the cliff height may increase

There may be forward slipping

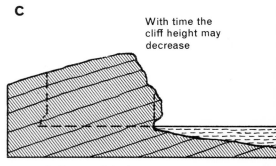

C

With time the cliff height may decrease

Collapse will be less drastic than in A

Fig. 223. The broken lines show successive positions of the cliff face.

Rock Structure

The composition, structure, and inclination of the rocks exposed in the cliffs obviously have much to do with the form of the cliff itself and the rate at which it recedes by erosion. Cliffs of loose, scarcely consolidated glacial material, like those in Fig. 175, may be worn back at a great rate; stretches of such coast in eastern England, when unprotected, were cut back by erosion at an average rate of five or six feet a year. Physically hard rocks may be much more resistant; but even then jointing may lead to disintegration and fairly rapid removal. Where, along the coast, harder rocks alternate with less resistant ones, they may come to form headlands and thus become vulnerable to attack on three sides (p. 128).

Terms like 'hard' and 'soft' are relative and should be used with caution. Besides which, a given rock may be compressed by folding and made more resistant to marine erosion, as the chalk of the Needles on the Isle of Wight.

The Dip of the Rocks

The cliff slopes and the dip of the rocks themselves are also important factors. Fig. 223 shows some of the ways in which such slopes may affect the steepness and rate of retreat of the coastline.

The slope of the cliffs and the dip of the strata need not necessarily coincide.

In Fig. 223, A and B show that the height of the cliffs may increase as they recede. At first they present a steep face to the sea, but other factors, such as weathering, may then lessen their slope. Also, the erosive action of the sea itself may become less as the cliffs recede and beach material accumulates (p. 133).

Example C shows that the present slope of a coastal landform may itself, in the long run, cause a decrease in cliff height.

The most regular coastlines resulting from erosion are generally those where the rocks are of uniform material, and not excessively jointed (Fig. 216).

The Wave-Cut Platform

As the cliffs are undercut and gradually worn back, a rocky foreshore is left, covered with varying amounts of beach material.

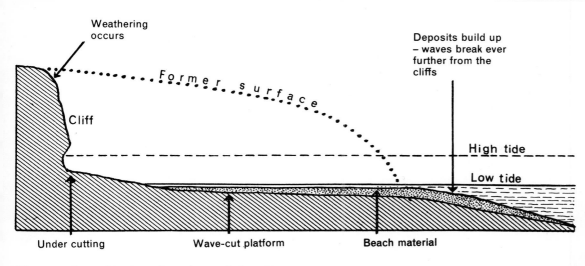

Fig. 224. A combination of erosion and deposition produces these typical coastal features.

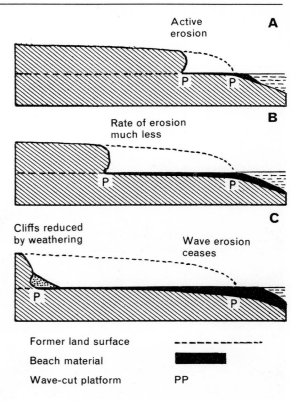

Former land surface   ----------

Beach material   ▬▬▬

Wave-cut platform   PP

Fig. 225. Shoreline development in the absence of uplift or submergence.

This is often exposed at low tide and forms what is known as a *wave-cut platform* (Fig. 224). As shingle and sand is washed back and forth over the surface, its irregularities may be abraded and smoothed, so that, with time, it tends to acquire a gentle seaward slope. Often steeply-dipping strata form corrugated ridges along the shore, their bedding planes clearly visible (Fig. 226).

Beach material from the cliffs, broken into ever smaller particles, tends to accumulate on the seaward parts of the platform, and in some cases to build up a gentle underwater profile off-shore. The development of a wave-cut platform and beach material depends on the nature of the coast itself. Sometimes the coastland plunges almost sheer into deep water. Also, uplift and submergence will prevent the balance depicted in Fig. 224 being achieved.

The Lessening of Wave Attack

Fig. 225 shows the change in the rate of erosion as a cliff is cut back.

As the wave-cut platform becomes wider, and the beach deposits cause a shallowing sea, the waves break far from the cliffs; even at high tide, or under storm conditions, they may lose the power to erode with anything like their former effectiveness. The rate of cliff retreat may then be slowed up.

It is as well to remember, however, that the whole process may not follow this course if there is rapid removal of beach debris, or if the cliffs themselves are of unconsolidated material.

Where this process has taken place, the cliffs may finally form a line of heights inland, where their slopes are lessened and heights lowered by long-continued weathering.

A change in sea level may later cause submergence of such a coast, and the old cliffs may retreat further under renewed wave attack.

The Wave-Cut Platform and the Dip of the Rocks

Fig. 226. The dip of these red sandstones at Watchet in Somerset has an influence on the shape of the headland, and, where the sea has planed off the wave-eroded rocks further out, the upper parts of the tilted strata can be seen through the covering of weed.

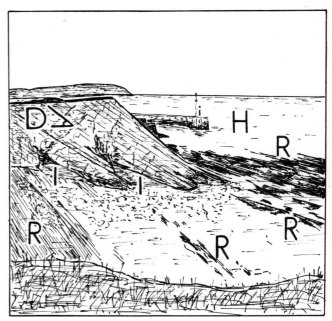

Fig. 227.

Notice the influence of the seaward dip of these red rocks on the shape of the headland, and on the nature of the inlets (I) and ridges (R), where the edges of the dipping strata are revealed on the wave-cut platform. The angle of dip is marked on the cliff face in Fig. 227.

Wave attack is still severe on the sides of the headland, for the range of the spring tides is very high in the Bristol Channel—as indicated by the markings on the harbour wall (H).

Beach Material and Cliff Structure

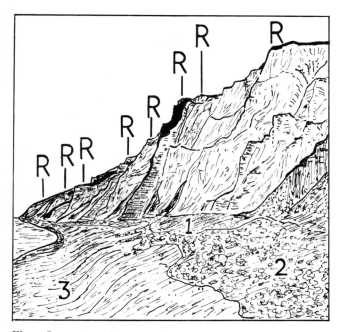

Fig. 228.

Fig. 229. Brightly coloured sands and clays make up the cliffs at Alum Bay in the Isle of Wight. These sedimentary rocks overlie the chalk, which is exposed further south, where the well-known wave-dissected ridge of the Needles is a chalk headland with stacks.

The loose cliff materials, mostly sands and clays, are easily eroded. Their bedding is vertical, and the different effects of weathering, rock fall, and slumping, in each case results in the ridging of the cliffs (RR) and the obvious variety of slopes and cliff levels.

Beneath the cliffs, the lighter coloured material (1) is made up partly of fallen rock and partly of beach deposits. Notice in the foreground chalk particles (2) transported from further along the coast, and thrown up by the waves.

At normal tides the waves are active mainly on the lower part of the shore (3), and to some extent the cliffs are protected from the full force of the waves at high tides by the beach deposits.

Coastlands

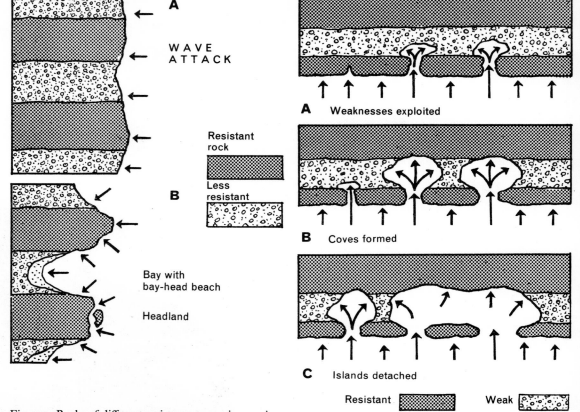

A broad classification of coasts may be made on the basis of their recent, or continuing, emergence or submergence. Features resulting from both processes are discussed on pp. 148-153, where it can be seen that much depends on whether the former coastline was highland or lowland.

The Lie of the Coastlands

The position of the existing hills and valleys relative to the shoreline is important, for drowning may produce tidal inlets, and cause renewed attacks on cliffs once more partly submerged. When these are nearly at *right-angles* to the shoreline, a 'capes and bays' type of coast is likely to be developed, and, if considerable submergence has occurred, a coastal landscape with deep inlets may result.

A clear example of this type of development may be seen near Swanage, in Dorset, where hard limestones, clays, chalk, and sands form hills and valleys at right-angles to the eastward facing coast. To the west of Swanage, however, on the south-facing coast, the same sequence of rocks lies

Fig. 230. Rocks of different resistance to marine erosion are at right-angles to the shoreline, each exposed to wave attack.

Fig. 231. The rocks of less resistance are only exposed to wave attack as the sea breaches those seaward of them.

parallel to the shore-line. There we see examples of the formation of the curved bays known as *coves*, formed by the erosion of soft rocks behind the barrier of Portland limestone, which the sea has breached (Figs. 232 and 233).

Fig. 231 shows, diagrammatically, the way in which the sea may surge through a breach in an outer, resistant rock, and more successfully erode less resistant ones inland. Waves soon create a cove behind the narrow inlet, but are less able to wear away the relatively resistant rocks further inland. Fig. 232 shows a late stage in the processes which lead to the formation of wider bays, with long islands close to the shore.

Cove Formation

For the purpose of observation, make a simple sketch map of this varied stretch of coast and mark on it:

1. The cove in the foreground.
2. The submerged platform.
3. The island remains of the outer, hard limestone.
4. Evidence of tight folding in this limestone.
5. The line of the weaker Greensand.
6. Rock fall.
7. Caves in the chalk.
8. Where the chalk cliff has already broken away and slipped downwards.

Notice that beyond the headland of hard limestone the outer rocks have been completely removed, leaving a chalk headland further along the coast, and a fairly uniform line of cliffs with valleys ending abruptly at the shore-line. Notice, also, the smoothness of the chalk Downs, with a lack of surface channels.

Fig. 232. Looking towards Durdle Door and Bat's Head, one sees the western limits of the succession of hard limestone, Greensand, and chalk which lie closely parallel to one another and to the shoreline, and an illustration of typical cove formation and amalgamation.

Cove Formation

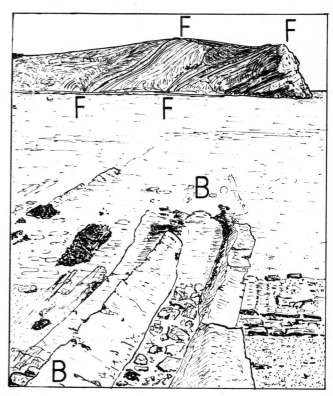

Fig. 234.

Fig. 233 shows the entrance to a cove, formed where softer rocks lie behind a resistant barrier of hard Portland limestones, which dip northwards (FF). Notice the steep dip of the beds (BB) in the foreground, continuations of those across the bay. These rocks protected a narrowing belt of sands and clays, which, after the breach, has been widened to form the cove itself. Inland the inlet is backed by steep chalk cliffs.

Fig. 233. The entrance to Lulworth Cove in Dorset.

The Drowning of a 'Dalmatian' Coast

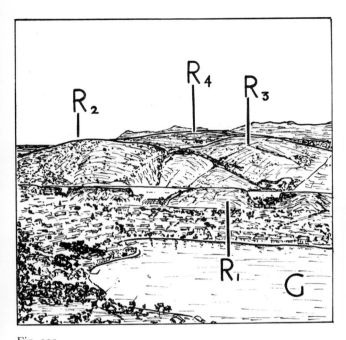

Fig. 235.

Fig. 236. The drowning of this part of the Dalmatian region of Jugoslavia (by a combination of subsidence and rising sea-level) has formed inlets of the sea between the lower of the parallel ridges of limestone. The small town of Bokarski Zaljev, with its tiny harbour, is typical of the settlements, restricted to the valleys.

This series of limestone ridges is part of the Dinaric mountain system, with folds running parallel with the Adriatic coast of Jugoslavia. Long valleys lie between the ridges R_1, R_2, R_3, R_4.

This drowned coastal region is thus a series of gulfs (G), peninsulas, and long narrow islands, the remnants of the partly submerged lower ridges.

The hinterland is part of the dry limestone highlands of the Karst, whose typical features are described on p. 24. Settlement is concentrated on the narrow coastal strips and lower pockets of land, known as the *primorje*.

Depositional Features

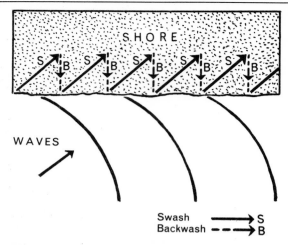

Fig. 237. Longshore drift where the wavefront arrives obliquely.

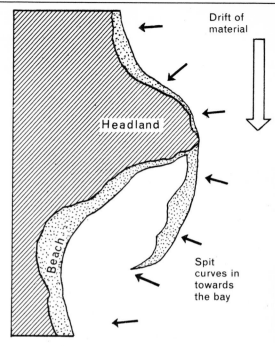

Fig. 238. Curved spit and a bayhead beach.

Deposition

Material eroded from the coast may be removed by backwash, undertow, and sea currents, perhaps to be deposited elsewhere; or waves may move it back and forth, so that it grinds itself down, by the process called *attrition*, into smaller and smaller particles; or it may be swept up the shore and left stranded as beach material.

The swash tends to carry material up the beach, and if the waves approach the coast at an oblique angle, they may move it steadily along the shore. Fig. 237 shows that the backwash recedes, under gravity, straight down the slope, so that as the next wave may again shift the material obliquely, a *longshore drift* of sand and shingle may take place. Man may have to construct groynes (Fig. 175) to check the movement of such material along the shore.

'Constructive' waves approaching the coast at right angles tend to build beach material into ridges parallel to the shore.

140

Storm Beaches and Dunes

In storms, when the waves are more powerful and higher than usual, heavy pebbles and other debris may be flung far up the shore, so that, under normal tidal conditions they are beyond the reach of the waves. Thus, in time, a high pebble ridge, or *storm beach* may develop (Fig. 244), capable of interfering with the land drainage (Figs. 59-62).

On sandy beaches, above the high tide mark, the particles may be carried further inshore by the wind, so that they eventually accumulate in the form of coarse dunes, which may move further inland or become 'fixed' by vegetation.

Bay-head Beaches

In the bays, wave action is usually not as powerful as it is on the adjoining headlands (Fig. 212); and on gently shelving bays, in particular, there tends to be much deposition, with the formation of a wide *bayhead beach*.

Spits and Bars

Where there is marked longshore drift, a low ridge of sand and pebbles may extend from a headland across a bay, usually curved towards the coast where the waves swing inwards as they enter the bay (Fig. 238).

Spits also tend to form where longshore currents carry material across a river mouth, so that much deposition occurs in slack water between the current and the main stream of the river. If a shingle spit of heavy material extends sufficiently far across the mouth, the river outlet may be diverted (Fig. 239).

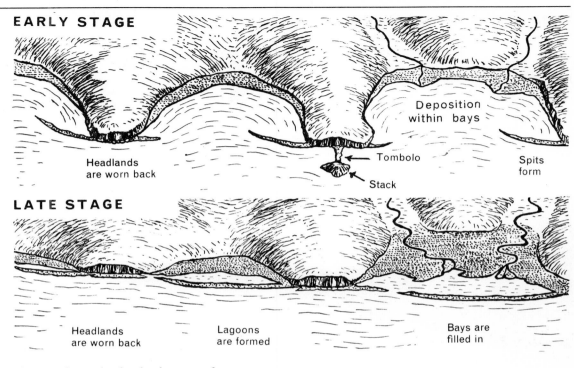

EARLY STAGE

Headlands
are worn back

Deposition
within bays

Tombolo

Stack

Spits
form

LATE STAGE

Headlands
are worn back

Lagoons
are formed

Bays are
filled in

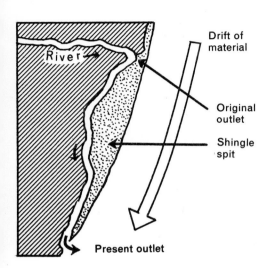

Drift of
material

River

Original
outlet

Shingle
spit

Present outlet

Fig. 239. The diversion of a river's outlet by marine deposition.

Fig. 240. Stages in the development of a more even shoreline through erosion and deposition.

An *offshore bar* may sometimes develop parallel to the shore, often by a combination of beach scouring, by backwash and undertow; in shallow seas a bar may be formed by deposition ahead of where the waves are breaking, some way offshore. This, too, may eventually come to extend across a bay.

A spit which extends so far that it links two headlands, is called a *bay-bar*, and may enclose a *lagoon*. Sometimes an island is linked to the mainland by a connecting bar, which is then called a *tombolo* (Fig. 250).

Shallowing coasts are most likely to have offshore bars of one form or another (Fig. 260).

Mud-Flats

In gently shelving sheltered coastal areas, especially in estuaries and bays, the tides may leave fine silt, and rivers add their alluvium, to build up broad mud-flats and create marshland. Salt-tolerant forms of vegetation tend to spread and cover the flat ground, through which wind muddy, tidal channels. Morecambe Bay in Lancashire has good examples, and see also p. 153.

Straightening the Coastline

Fig. 240 shows how the long-continuing processes of erosion and deposition can act to cut back headlands and also fill in the bays behind by marine deposition, with the aid of sediments from streams and rivers. The coastline as a whole, thus tends to become straighter.

Though it is possible for these processes to produce an even shoreline, in most cases the relative changes of land and sea level, with drowning or emergence, are apt to interrupt the sequence and create new coastal landforms.

Coastal Deposition

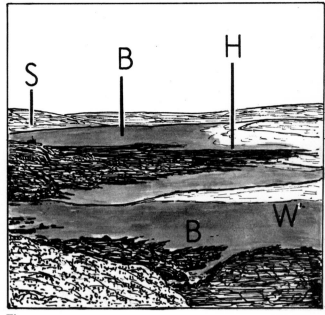

Fig. 242.

Fig. 242. The North Devon coast near Mortehoe, to the west of Exmoor, where the shoreline runs more or less at right-angles across alternating beds of hard and soft rocks—slates, hard grits, and softer sandstones—giving a 'capes and bays' type of coast (p. 136).

The harder beds (H) project as headlands, between which softer rocks (S) have been rapidly cut back to form the bays. Gently sloping beaches (B) have been built up within the bays, and the wave-attack on the softer rocks behind has been lessened as a result.

The smaller inlets in the harder, slaty rocks in the foreground are due to the erosion of structural weaknesses within these rocks. Streams from inland form drainage channels across the bays, and, like the watercourse (W), may flow fast and cut into the sands at low tide.

Storm Beaches

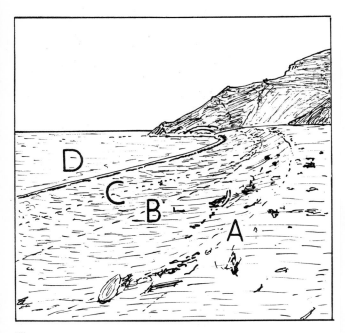

Fig. 243.

Prominent ridges A, B, C show how the waves at successive exceptionally high tides have thrown tons of pebbles onto the beach. High tides and severe storms have caused waves to cast up the debris, seen littered, stranded, like the pebbles, at the highest level.

Many of the pebbles, though smoothed, are very flat. These are mostly derived from the shaly rocks of parts of the adjoining coasts.

The line of weed at D shows the highest position of the present tides; at which stage, of course, the waves can do little to affect most of this long storm beach, although its profile changes with exceptionally high tides. (See also Fig. 59).

Fig. 244. The high barrier-beach running from Hurlstone Point, in the background, around the wide Porlock Bay in west Somerset. Behind it lies areas of marsh and small lagoons, and, beyond, the Vale of Porlock.

143

Cliff Destruction by Weathering and Erosion

Make an outline sketch and on it identify the following features:
1. The effects of slumping.
2. Scree slopes.
3. Contrasting angles of slope due to varying rock resistance.
4. A steep transverse valley running down to shore level (and suggest reasons for its presence).
5. Rock falls.
6. A stack.

Comment on the nature of the beach and the shoreline, and on the role of the sea in causing this type of landscape.

Compare the nature of this coast with that in another part of the Isle of Wight (Fig. 229), and suggest reasons for the differences in their appearance.

Fig. 245. Dramatic coastal scenery at Blackgang on the Isle of Wight. The seaside house in the foreground has been completely destroyed, and the cliffs show some remarkable contrasts in movements of rocks and soils.

The Effects of Erosion and Deposition

Again construct an outline sketch, and mark on it the following features:

1. A headland.
2. A bayhead beach.
3. Part of a wave-cut platform.
4. Places where agents other than waves are acting to modify the coastal scenery. Explain exactly how such agents act to alter the appearance of the cliffs.

Consider how the exposed rocks illustrate the terms 'bedding', and 'dip', and show this diagrammatically.

Comment on the influence of the rocks and their bedding on the coastal features.

Suggest reasons why there is such a marked change in the coastline at the head of the bay.

Fig. 246. The action of the sea on Carboniferous strata at Newgale Sands on the Pembrokeshire coast, where the shoreline and the edge of the low plateau show the combined effects of erosion, deposition, and weathering.

Deposition: Spit Formation and Lagoons

Fig. 247. A fine example of a long, curving shingle ridge, near Slapton in south Devon. Nearly two miles long, it separates the freshwater lake (L), Slapton Ley, from the sea.

Fig. 248.

As in Fig. 244 there are well-marked wave-formed ridges of beach deposits, R_1, R_2, R_3. The line of houses and the road emphasise the size and relative permanence of the feature.

The separation of a lagoon from the open sea is generally followed by its eventual infilling by deposition from streams. In some cases the lagoon may be narrowed as material from the ridge is carried landward by exceptional storms and waves at high tides. Thus in each case the formation of a complete bar may act to straighten the coastline.

Even the long Chesil Beach, in Dorset, over forty feet high in places, is migrating slowly towards the land and narrowing the tidal lagoon, the Fleet.

Deposition: A Linking Tombolo

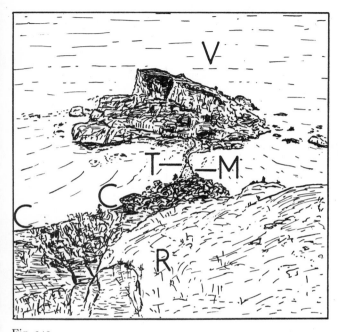

Fig. 249.

Fig. 250. A mass of volcanic rock (V) lies close to the Sicilian shore of the Straits of Messina; like the rocky slopes (R) in the foreground, it is material ejected from one or other of the cones of the great composite volcanic mass, Mt. Etna. It is linked to the shore by a shingle ridge known as a tombolo.

Here a spit has built out from the mainland beach, which curves in the foreground (CC) to a headland below the dark mass of trees. On the island is another beach of coarse volcanic particles, and between the two is the long linking bar, or *tombolo* (T).

The waves can be seen moving onto each side of the ridge of shingle, which is also derived from the volcanic rocks along the coast. The island lies almost at the mid-point of the shoreline of a gently curving bay, and wave fronts which approach the island parallel to one another swing inwards as they advance beyond it. The figure of the man (M) gives a scale to the tombolo which is built up by the waves.

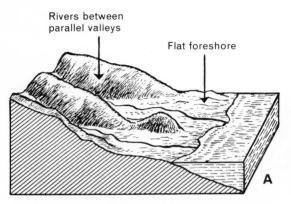

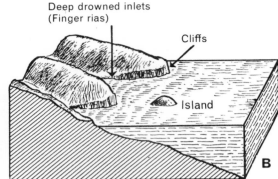

Fig. 251. Tidal inlets and new cliffs formed after submergence.

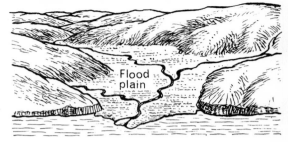

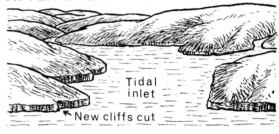

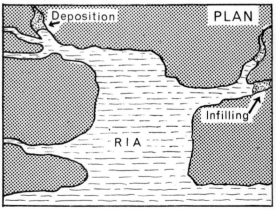

Fig. 252. Drowned river valleys.

Changes of Land/Sea Level

Movements of the earth's crust may cause the land surface locally to rise or sink, relative to the existing sea-level, perhaps as *isostatic* adjustments to glaciation (see p. 101). Such movements may be very local in effect, or widespread over a particular part of the earth's surface.

On the other hand there may be a world-wide change in sea-level. This may slowly fall relative to the land as when, for instance, water is 'locked up' in the form of ice during a prolonged Ice Age. Conversely, the level may rise when melt-water returns once more to ocean circulation as milder conditions prevail. Such general changes are said to be *eustatic*.

Whatever the cause, there can thus be periods during which the land surface becomes higher, relative to the sea, and coastlands emerge; and other periods when widespread drowning occurs and many coastal features become submerged.

More locally, stretches of the coast may be lifted from the sea; relatively recent uplifts have occurred in parts of New Zealand and central Chile together with violent earthquakes.

Shorelines of Submergence

In general, the drowning of a highland zone bordering the sea causes new, steep, cliffs to be formed. Valleys between highland ridges may become deep inlets. Fig. 251B shows these coastal features in their early stages.

Submerged river valleys become long, winding inlets, known as *rias*. The deep inlets of England's south-western peninsula, and the long Milford Haven in South Wales are the result of such drowning, forming deep tidal estuaries extending far inland, with obvious benefits for shipping and trade. Fig. 252 shows the creation of a tidal inlet, with marine erosion within the valley.

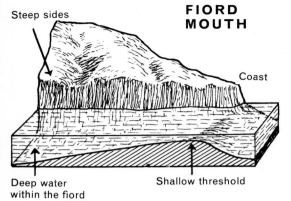

FIORD MOUTH

Steep sides

Coast

Deep water within the fiord

Shallow threshold

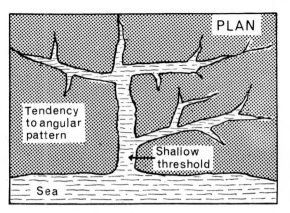

PLAN

Tendency to angular pattern

Shallow threshold

Sea

Fig. 253. The drowning of glacially overdeepened valleys.

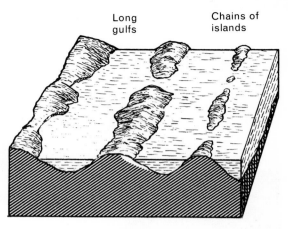

Long gulfs

Chains of islands

Fig. 254. Parallel folds partly submerged by the rising sea.

Rias usually have the natural winding course of the former river valley. The main river and its tributaries deposit alluvium at the head of the drowned part of the valleys, where their flow meets the deeper water, now fairly far inland. This accumulates, and at low tide extensive mud flats may be exposed. Nearer the sea, waves begin to cut new cliffs on the shores of the ria and along the drowned coast.

Fiords

Some glacially over-deepened U-shaped valleys extend to the coast, and have subsequently been drowned; so that they, too, form long, very deep inlets, called *fiords*. They present a different appearance, and have a different long profile to the normal ria.

The valley spurs have generally been truncated, so that drowning has created long, almost straight stretches of water along the valley. For much of their length, the valley sides plunge steeply into

deep water. But near the mouth, where the valley was not deepened to the same extent, a ridge, sometimes exposed, sometimes bearing moraine, more usually covered by water, gives a shallow 'threshold' approach from the sea.

The straightness of the main valley and glaciated tributaries tend to give fiord systems an angularity, which may be partly due to the influence of faults on the pattern of the original valleys.

Most of the fiord coastlands are on the west side of the continents in the cool, or cold, temperate latitudes, where, today, rainfall totals are large. During the Ice Ages snowfall would have been heavy, so that powerful mountain glaciers descended to low altitudes. Notice the location of the fiord coasts of northern Norway, north-west Scotland, south-west New Zealand, British Columbia, and southern Chile. Such powerful erosion has produced very deep water in the inner parts—up to 4,000 ft. deep in some Norwegian fiords. Infilling may occur at the valley head, though they quickly become deep.

'Dalmatian' Coastlands

Fig. 254 shows that, as along the Jugoslav Dalmatian coast, submergence of hills and valleys formed by folds parallel to the shoreline may give rise to numerous long gulfs and off-shore islands (see also Fig. 236). Cork harbour has been formed in this way. As with other submerged highland coasts a 'youthfulness' results, in that marine erosion now begins to create new steep cliffs.

Submergence of Coastal Lowlands

Rising sea-level may cause the drowning of a large area of a lowland coast. Much deposition occurs in the shallow waters, and offshore bars tend to form, holding back silt. The results are that marshes and mudflats form, exposed at low-tide, and also shallow shifting inlets or broad, shallow estuaries. In time the deposition, with the help of vegetation, extends the land area again, by filling in the broad inlets formed by submergence and so straightening the coastline. Such developments can be seen, in stages, on the Suffolk coast.

149

Drowned Inlet: A Fiord

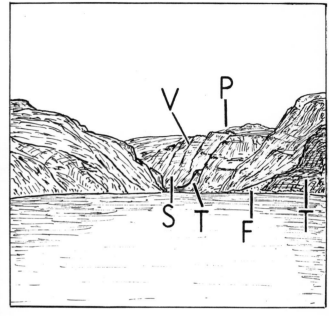

Fig. 256.

Fig. 255. The head of a deep fiord in western Norway. A valley was cut into the plateau P by river action, and, later, glaciers deepened and widened it. It extended to the coast, and so a subsequent rise in sea-level drowned the valley to form a long inlet, very deep in its much eroded middle reaches.

Notice the river-dissected plateau (P), and also the truncated spurs (T). The latter formerly extended partly across the valley, but were worn back by the moving ice of a glacier—giving a straightened stretch, characteristic of fiords.

The angle of the upper slopes indicated at V is that of the sides of the former river valley. Notice the steeper slopes of the truncated spurs below. In fact, a scree slope (S) masks the break of slope further up the valley. Another slope of recently formed rock debris, possibly partly washed down, has collected as a fan at F.

The Estuary of a Drowned River System: A Ria

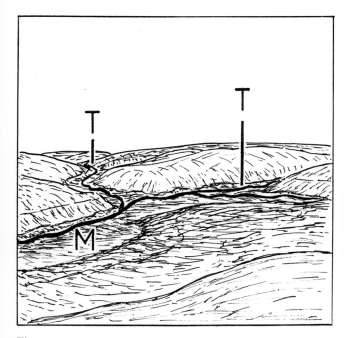

Fig. 257.

The tidal waters have risen, and now cover the valleys of the main river (M) and its tributaries (T). Thus a system of rias occupies the winding valleys of the former rivers. The main channel becomes deeper as it approaches the sea; but in the part of the Porthcuel ria shown, low tide exposes extensive mud flats.

Fig. 257 shows, diagrammatically, the former streams in their floodplains. Minor streams would then have been more active in cutting into the countryside; but with rising waters the fall to base-level decreases (p. 33), so that much deposition takes place at the upper, tidal limits of these drowned valleys.

Fig. 258. A system of drowned river valleys (rias) extends into the low, dissected plateau of south-east Cornwall. Here, near St. Mawes, the main Porthcuel River flows towards the estuary of the Fal ria.

Shorelines of Emergence

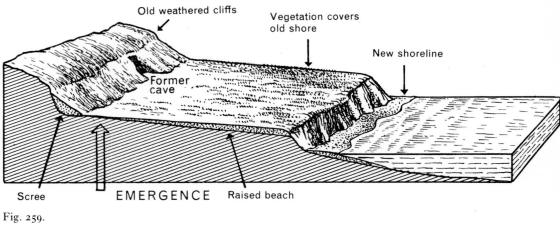

Fig. 259.

Emergent Coasts

With the post-glacial rise in sea levels, coasts of submergence are now more common than those of emergence. Nevertheless, there is plenty of evidence of periods of emergence in the past. Today, low-lying coasts are most likely to reveal emergence, for uplift of a few feet can affect a large area of coastal flats.

Emergence and Shore Features

Where coastlands are lifted and emerge slowly from the sea, a gently sloping off-shore shelf will be exposed and form a new shore, covered with the marine debris already deposited upon it. (Fig. 259).

The former beach with its sand and shingle and the wave-cut cliffs behind may also be raised, so that they are no longer directly affected by sea action. Where the wave-cut platform once sloped down to the sea, it now stands as a long shelf, and beneath it the new cliffs are in turn cut back by

152

present marine erosion.

The old cliffs, now well inland, are acted on by agents of weathering, so that their angle of slope is gradually reduced.

Frequent, but irregular, uplift may occur in regions where movements of the earth's crust are common, as in the lands bordering the Mediterranean sea. In other regions there may be periods of more general uplift, like those occurring in the lands of northern Europe which once bore the weight of massive ice sheets and are now adjusting themselves to the removal of this great burden. In any locality there may in time be several phases of uplift. In all these cases, raised beaches may be identified at various heights—the older usually showing more clearly the effects of weathering and erosion. Sometimes only the traces of beaches at expected heights can be identified.

A falling of sea-level and the drying up of inland seas and lakes may also leave elevated shorelines about their perimeter. It is not, in fact, always

easy to tell whether in the past the land had risen or the sea-level fallen.

Emergence and Off-shore Features

Fig. 260A shows how the waves, breaking far from the shore on a shallow, emerging coastal shelf, can build up an off-shore bar, especially where currents carry a fairly heavy load.

Between the bar and the shore, land deposits accumulate, and when a complete barrier beach is well established (B), tend to fill in the lagoon behind, and so create conditions which favour marshes. Winds and waves may move the barrier steadily in towards the shore. Thus, with the materials carried down from the land and the lagoon narrowed by the encroaching bar, a new type of shoreline develops, fringed with marshes and dunes (C). Eventually there may be just a zone of sandy ridges along the coast.

Such features are to be seen along the emergent coasts of the south-eastern U.S.A.

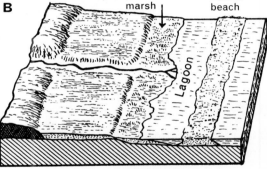

A

Old cliffs

Coastal plain emerging

Bar forming

Low cliff – nip

Incised stream

Shallowing

B

Deposits with marsh

Barrier beach

Lagoon

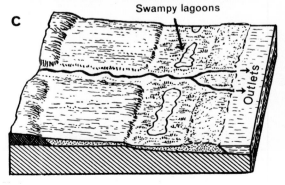

Swampy lagoons

C

Outlets

Fig. 260. A new coastline created by deposition on a shallowing shelf.

Rejuvenation

The processes which cause the uplift of the coastlands also cause the rivers and their tributaries draining the land surface to become more active. On the coastal plain the rivers cut downwards and their meanders are frequently incised.

The results are felt throughout the river system, and gradually the typical features of rejuvenation—the knick-points and terraces—become part of the valleys (pp. 60-61).

Coastal Vegetation

Vegetation plays such a big part in forming and consolidating new coastland that it is as well to consider its exact functions in this respect.

Close-rooting plants, like the mangrove vegetation (Fig. 269) growing in shallow coastal waters can trap silt, sand, and vegetable debris and so help a land surface develop.

In swamps, marsh plants may be the first to develop. They then help to build up the founda-

tions of soil from trapped mineral particles and vegetable remains, in which other plants may root themselves. Thus, gradually, a succession of more typical land plants can take over; eventually firm coastal land is formed.

Sandy areas, such as dunes formed of particles blown inland from marine deposits on the shore, may be 'fixed' by grasses, like marram grass, with long spreading roots.

On cliffed coasts vegetation may have a number of contrasting effects. As with dunes, a loose crumbling cliff of sandstone may be 'fixed' to some extent by a covering of grasses or by various climbing plants. On the other hand, trees which may take root on more resistant cliffs, in joints or on ledges of a hard rocky surface, may prove destructive as the roots widen cracks and loosen the cliff face.

Emergence: Barrier Beaches

Fig. 261. The coastland of southern Spain, between Algeciras and Malaga, shows many features resulting from recent uplift. Rivers like this enter the sea via waters ponded back (P) by deposition along the shore-line. In some cases, infilling behind bars has given fertile, reclaimed farmland.

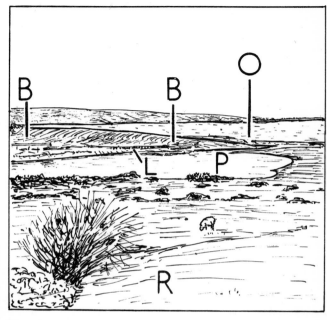

Fig. 262.

On an emergent coast, such as this, much material accumulates off-shore and is rolled in against the coast by the waves. The mouths of the rivers tend to be blocked by coastal deposits.

Here an old bar (BB) lies parallel with the shore. Inland are series of well marked raised beaches, of which only the lowest (R), in the foreground, appears in the picture.

The rivers are incised in the coastal lowland, and even here there are signs of river erosion at a former higher level (L). The narrow outlet (O) is cut through a combination of marine and alluvial deposits.

Emergence: Raised Beaches

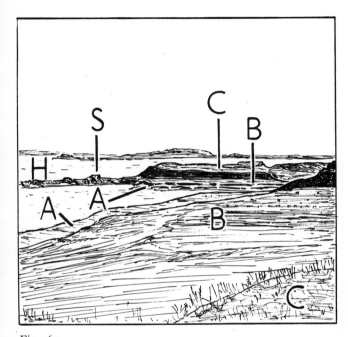

Fig. 263.

Three levels A, B, and C can be identified, and the sea is actively eroding cliffs below the edge of A, the lower of the raised beaches.

The remains of a former headland (H) can be seen, and when the land level was much lower, relatively, than today the hill S may well have stood out as a stack.

Though sea-levels have risen generally since the beginning of the last major retreat of the ice, here there has been an upward, isostatic, movement of the land. Two beaches, at approximately 25 feet and 100 feet, can be identified on many parts of this coast, formed when conditions remained static long enough for cliff retreat and beach formation.

Fig. 264. A series of plane surfaces at different levels, typical of the coastlands of western Scotland and the Western Isles. At the lower level are raised beaches, with the remains of former cliffs inland of them.

Reefs and Atolls

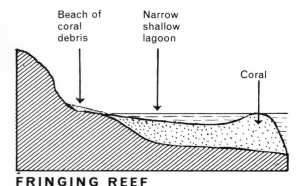

FRINGING REEF

Fig. 265A.

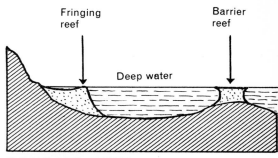

BARRIER REEF

Fig. 265B.

Coral

Tiny marine organisms called *polyps* are able to secrete lime obtained from sea-water and form a hard skeleton of calcium carbonate. Colonies of these live in clusters on rocks, or on the skeletal remains of former colonies, and so manage to build up masses of *coral*. Various algae also help to produce limy matter and encrust rocks and corals.

Different clusters of these minute organisms produce a variety of coral forms—branching corals, sponge-like, or brain-like masses, white or coloured (although few retain their brilliant colours when out of the water). When a large continuous mass builds upwards and outwards from a rock base, it is called a *reef*.

The Growth of Reefs

Corals are built up in sea-water, when the water temperature is about, or above, 20°C (68°F). This means that reefs are found along coasts between latitudes approximately 30°N and 25°S, especially on the eastern sides of continents, where the warmer currents flow close to the shores (p. 121). They cannot develop out of water, and therefore must be formed below low-tide level. The organisms thrive in clear water, down to about 30 fathoms, so that reefs are not found off muddy estuaries.

Waves tend to break pieces from the outer parts of the reefs, so that beaches of coarse, broken dazzling white coral particles are commonly built up inshore of the reefs.

Types of Reef

Coral platforms are built out from the coasts as *fringing reefs*, usually with a shallow lagoon between the outer, developing reef and the mainland. They are often particularly wide off the headlands, where the salt water is most likely to be clear.

Some reefs may be separated from the mainland, with its fringing reefs, by water which may be too deep for coral growth, and so form barriers a long way off-shore. These *barrier reefs* may lie in lines off-shore, separated from each other by deep channels, or may form irregular rings about an island.

Atolls

These are low-lying rings of coral islands, at or near sea-level, their outer beaches built up of coral fragments. Beyond these extend a shallow outer lagoon and a reef, almost exposed at low tide, which falls steeply to the ocean depths at the outer edge. On the inside of the islands and their inner beaches is a deep flat-floored lagoon.

There are several likely explanations of the origin of these atolls. Their coral formations rise from depths at which coral could not now be formed. The accumulation of such thicknesses must have involved either a slow rise in sea-level, with coral formation keeping pace, or else a

156

subsidence of the land to which it is attached.

The following are the outlines of two acceptable theories, the first by Darwin (since modified by considering a rising sea-level, rather than simply subsidence), the second by Daly. Together they account for most of the characteristics of atolls.

Fig. 266A shows a fringing reef formed about an oceanic island. As the land subsided, or sea-level rose (as it has done with the melting of former extensive ice sheets) corals have built upwards and outwards (B). Broken coral provides a flat floor for the inner lagoon, which may be 40 or 50 fathoms deep. Breaks between the islands, in some cases deep channels, possibly occur where the original reefs were incomplete.

Another possibility is that when sea-levels were much lower, the islands with their reefs were reduced by erosion to wave-cut platforms. As the sea-level rose, renewed coral growth took place, upwards and outwards, perhaps a foot each 10-20 years, about the fringe of the flat platform.

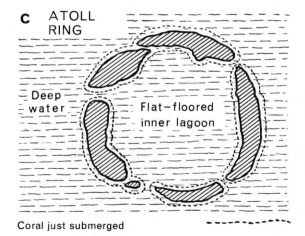

C ATOLL RING

Deep water

Flat-floored inner lagoon

Coral just submerged

Fig. 266. Continued coral growth during land subsidence or rising sea-level.

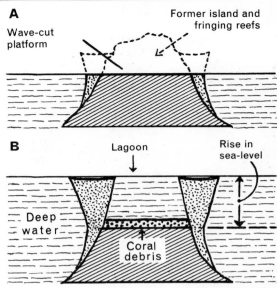

A
Wave-cut platform
Former island and fringing reefs

B
Lagoon
Rise in sea-level
Deep water
Coral debris

Fig. 267. Renewed coral growth in rising waters after plantation during a period of low sea-levels.

Raised Reefs and Fossil Corals

Raised coral platforms are found in many parts of the world. 'Living' reefs, of course, cannot grow above the tidal level, and so these 'dead, and usually discoloured, limestone platforms are studied as reliable indications of vertical coastal movements. Examples are seen in Jamaica (Fig. 268) and along the Kenya coastlands (p. 158).

Reef-building corals existed in early Palaeozoic times, and fossil reefs are found among rocks formed hundreds of millions of years ago. They are useful indicators of past climates. By piecing together world-wide evidence, and assuming that conditions required by early corals were much the same as those in which present corals flourish, deductions may be made about the movements of ancient landmasses and 'continental drift'.

157

Reefs and Raised Coral

There are many raised reefs and narrow coral terraces about the shores of Jamaica, showing that there have been a number of small recent uplifts.

The colour of most of these is now a light buff, and few corals maintain a vivid colour out of water. The old reefs themselves are, of course, being eroded by the waves, and most of the beaches have a covering of light coral sand, with particles from the other rocks which form the headlands.

Raised coral platforms are reliable indicators of uplift by earth movements. Along the shores of the Indian Ocean in Kenya, a level coral surface has been uplifted and forms a steeply cliffed coastal platform extending for many miles along the coast northwards of Mombasa, itself on an island which is part of the raised surface. The coral provides, amongst other things, material for large cement works. Conditions are still suitable for coral formation, so that off-shore new reefs of live coral flourish, except where rivers bring down fresh water, silt, and mud.

Fig. 268. Coconut palms grow on raised coral on the north-western shores of Jamaica. Several of the beautiful bays on the north coast lie almost enclosed by raised reefs, some of which, detached by wave action, form small off-shore islands.

Mangrove Vegetation

Notice the many stilt roots of the mangroves extending into the mud, sand, and salt water of the bay. The establishment and spread of the trees encourage the development of new land along the coast. The roots allow silt to build up and trap larger particles and plant remains.

As the soils become consolidated, the various species of trees which make up the mangrove vegetation may be gradually replaced by others which have established themselves among them. Palms, like that to the right of the picture, are among such trees: the tall coconut palm beyond, however, is growing on part of an eroded coral reef, which can just be seen beyond the mangroves.

Some mangroves produce seeds which germinate and form long dart-like plumules which, on breaking away, fall and stick into the silt beneath. Thus many new plants develop just beyond the parent trees.

The term 'mangrove' is, in fact, used to describe many shrubs and trees with some of these characteristics, and with the ability to live under conditions existing along tropical tidal shores and inlets.

Fig. 269. Mangroves growing along the shore near Port Antonio in northern Jamaica.

Index

Index of Place Names